Socialization to Civil Society

Socialization to Civil Society

A Life-History Study of Community Leaders

Peter Robert Sawyer

STATE UNIVERSITY OF NEW YORK PRESS

Published by
State University of New York Press, Albany

For information, address State University of New York Press,
90 State Street, Suite 700, ALbany, NY 12207

Production by Michael Haggett
Marketing by Susan M. Petrie

Library of Congress Cataloging-in-Publication Data

Sawyer, Peter Robert.
    Socialization to civil society : a life-history study of community leaders / Peter
Robert Sawyer.
        p. cm.
    Includes bibliographical references and index.
    ISBN 0-7914-6185-8 (hardcover : alk. paper) — ISBN 0-7914-6186-6 (pbk. : alk.
paper)
    1. Community leadership.   2. Civic leaders.   I. Title.

HM781.S39   2004
303.3'2—dc22
                                                                            2004018696

10 9 8 7 6 5 4 3 2 1

Contents

v

Preface

This book is dedicated to the real heroes of today, those who commit their time and energy to their families and communities. Without them, no democratic society will survive for long.

My thanks go to the subjects in this book for their time and for their fine example. I would also like to thank all of the teachers and fellow students along my academic path. They provided tremendous intellectual engagement regarding the problems and possibilities of democratic life. Among the faculty at Syracuse University, I would like to acknowledge Ralph Ketcham, Gerald Grant, Robert Bogdan, and Richard Braungart for their dedication to teaching and for all of their support on this project.

I would like to thank my friends and family who have endured my constant need to discuss many of the topics in this book. Throughout the years, the places, and the times, they have helped me think more deeply about the world and the variety of views and experiences that can be brought to it. I would also like to thank my children, Wyatt and Zachary. I am very grateful to have had them with me during the completion of this project. While sacrificing some of our time together, they have never been far from my heart, nor from my thoughts.

Chapter 1

Strengthening Civil Society

Civil society[1] has been cast as the vibrant core of modern democracy. In *Making Democracy Work: Civic Traditions in Modern Italy* (1993), Robert Putnam suggests that civil society, or *civil communities*, should resolve problems of collective action[2] and encourage modern democratic institutions to function successfully. His detailed statistical analysis supports his central claim that civil society and individual engagement in civil society result in strengthening local government. Individuals who participate in various mediating institutions within civil society become more knowledgeable about their communities, their local governments, and their political representatives. They also tend to have a higher degree of social trust, or *social capital*, and they tend to participate in politics of "public issues" rather than politics based on "personal advantage" (Putnam, 1993, p. 96). These findings reflect those of Verba, Schlozman, and Brady (1995) in the United States, who found that engagement in civil society "provide[s] additional opportunities for the acquisition of politically relevant resources and the enhancement of a sense of psychological engagement with politics" (p. 4). Both of these studies provide a clear understanding of what civil society does for local, regional, and national government, however, both fail to provide us with an understanding of how individuals are socialized into participating in civil society.

Charles Derber (1996) also makes the claim that civil society is important to American democracy, but like Putnam, he fails to adequately discuss how individuals become engaged in civil society. What Derber does offer is a critique of the modern liberal state and its focus on the individual which, as he argues, leads to *wilding*.

> Wilding includes a vast spectrum of self-centered and self-aggrandizing behavior that harms others. A wilding epidemic tears at the social fabric and

1

threatens to unravel society itself, ultimately reflecting the erosion of the moral order and the withdrawal of feelings and commitments from others to oneself, to "number one." (p. 6)

Democracy, according to Derber, is "the best antidote for wilding" (1996, p. 165). He argues, particularly, that the traditions of American civil society can counteract the warped sense of individualism that leads to wilding.

Civil society is the underlying antidote the wilding virus, involving a culture of love, morality, and trust that leads people to care for one another and for the larger community. A civil society's institutions nurture civic responsibility by providing incentives for people to act not just in their own interest but for the common good. (p. 145)

Fundamental to Putnam's and Derber's positions is the belief that individuals who engage themselves in civil society learn to pursue self-interest within a broader notion of public life. In resolving problems of collective action and in realizing civic responsibility, each citizen must be able to see his or her private life within a context of larger public concerns, concerns that reach beyond the direct needs of the individual.

The ability to conceptualize private self-interest within public life is best referred to as *enlightened self-interest* (Tussman, 1997). Enlightened self-interest does not refer to altruistic behavior but "is what one would want if he [or she] is wise, or far-sighted, or mature, or 'social'" (Tussman, 1997, p. 107). Through a direct look into the lives of individuals engaged in civil society, this book provides evidence that enlightened self-interest and engagement in civil society reinforce one another.

Unfortunately, American society is leaning away from participation within civil society, particularly participation related to one's own community. Alexis de Tocqueville anticipated this decrease of participation in civil society due to the unique perspective of American individualism. While early American society relied on civil society for economic cooperation and political order, de Tocqueville believed that the unique emphasis of American individualism would, in time, erode engagement in community life (de Tocqueville, 1848/1990). In a similar vein, many contemporary writers such as Bellah, Madsen, Sullivan, Swidler, and Tipton (1992) and Benjamin Barber (1995), along with those writers who are identified as communitarians (Etzioni, 1996; Walzer, 1995; Sandel, 1996), also argue that individualism and liberalism have led to a devaluation of community life. They state that individualism has become incorporated into the larger mechanisms of the modern market and state, and that these mechanisms have left little room for civil society.

While some deterioration of civil society can be found throughout American society, that deterioration is not complete. This book focuses on one community in which civic participation continues to be an important part of social life. This community has many members who are significantly involved in the welfare of their town. Their life histories provide some understanding to the unanswered question of how individuals become engaged in civil society.

Until recently, little attention has been paid to civil society, a surprising circumstance given its importance to successful democratic institutions. Perhaps the recent interest in civil society and the recognition of its importance to American democracy reflect the steadily increasing tension between the individual and larger structures of public life. While individual rights have continually expanded (Marshall, 1965), we have failed to provide a public context in which these rights are to be exercised (Etzioni, 1996). The Lockean liberal traditions that have dominated our society have also dominated our research. Research on civil society has been limited due, in part, to the structure of funding and the influence of the free market system (Ansley & Gaventa, 1997). In fact, researchers have focused on the very social formations that compete with civil society, including the free market system and the mechanisms of the state (Walzer, 1995).

When one examines the political socialization of citizen involvement, little beyond the social movement literature of the 1960s can be found to explain spontaneous civic engagement. Most of the literature on political socialization either refers to voting behavior or describes political participation as "activity that is intended to or has the consequence of affecting, either directly or indirectly, government action" (Verba, Schlozman, & Brady, 1995, p. 9). While much of civil society does indeed have an impact on governmental action, its true value is the ability of people to resolve public problems without the intrusion of government agencies or large market mechanisms.

While not directly in the field of political socialization, there are some books that do relate well to this work and to some of the social movement literature of the sixties. These books also focus on the lives of citizen models. The models they use are somewhat different, however, but their findings support and enhance the findings in this book.

The first book, *Common Fire: Leading Lives of Commitment in a Complex World*, is most closely related in its approach and results. The authors researched the lives of 100 people who had "sustained long-term commitments to work on behalf of the common good" (Daloz, Keen, Keen, & Parks, 1996, p. 5). The extent of civic commitment generally is beyond that of the citizens researched in this book. Similarly, *Soul of a Citizen: Living with Conviction in a Cynical Time*, by Paul Rogat Loeb, and *Local Heroes: The Rebirth of Heroism in America*, by Bill Berkowitz, also focus on exceptional commitments to social justice and the common good. These commitments tend to dominate the lives of these citizens, while the lives of the citizens examined here maintain commitments to other jobs and careers as well as, like some of the subjects in all of these studies, to family life.

Their findings, and their focus on what could be called "extraordinary citizenship," may be the next step in understanding citizen involvement in civil society. Interestingly enough, however, many of the subject descriptions offered by these studies and their subjects' experiences during childhood are very similar to what we found here. These other subjects, particularly in the book *Common Fire*, seem to have developed a higher level of moral commitment to social justice and a more dominating idea of a civic career. In any case, their findings are tied into the findings presented in chapters 5 and 6.

While not all of these studies focus on involvement in one's own community, this book explores civil society within the subjects' specific community and describes and explains the motivations, identities, and experiences of those people who are engaged in community life. These descriptions and explanations provide some evidence for how citizens come to be engaged in civil society, and how civil society relates to enlightened self-interest. The citizens selected for this research were involved in mediating institutions in the community and had a reputation of having enlightened self-interest. They were asked for their theories of public life within the community, their life histories to explain their political socialization, and their own descriptions of their identity.

The practical outcomes of this research are to identify patterns of socialization occurring in social institutions such as family, school, work, and neighborhood that may influence young people to become more engaged in civil society. The discovery of these patterns may help us construct and support social institutions in ways that promote civic involvement in community life and reinforce civic action based on enlightened self-interest.

The second and third chapters of this book outline some of the important issues related to citizenship and citizen involvement and delineate conceptions of civil society and political socialization. Chapter 2 introduces the concepts of civil society and mediating institutions. It includes a brief history of civil society and a specific section on civil society in the United States. It also examines the importance of civil society to democracy and the differing perspectives one may take on civil society.

The third chapter briefly describes the field of political socialization, its problems as a field of study and the relevant research. Chapter 3 defines the major agents of political socialization and provides an overview of the research that informs the question of how citizens are socialized for engagement in civil society. The chapter also presents Verba, Schlozman, and Brady's (1995) view that civil society leads to greater involvement in political society and concludes with some general suggestions for theory and research in this field.

Chapter 4 provides a detailed description of the methods used in this research. This chapter extends the previous one and summarizes the expectations for research. The chapter discusses the social research practices used in this study, including the site and subject selection, the life history method, and community studies, and it identifies the significant explanatory variables. Brief biographies of each of these subjects are available in appendix D. The entire research process is outlined and concludes with a description of the analysis used to generate the results.

Chapter 5 provides the results of the study. It examines the model citizens in terms of their values, norms, motivations, political concepts, and ideas regarding community involvement. Along with political concepts, each subject's beliefs about how problems are resolved within the community are also presented. In this and in chapter 6, extensive quotes are used to provide the context for subjects' comments and to allow the reader an opportunity for further analysis.

Chapter 6 examines the patterns in the socialization of these civic-minded people. Generational differences, gender, and residential patterns are incorporated into these discussions. The research findings provided in these chapters are contextualized within the broader literature of the field of political socialization.

Chapter 7 uses the findings in this study to provide practical suggestions for enhancing civic responsibility and participation in civil society through various institutional settings. This chapter also points out some of the problems and shortcomings of this research and the possibilities for future research in political socialization.

Conducting research on socialization to civil society is imperative to the democratic ideals of the United States and other modern democracies. With the growth of dysfunctional individualism and the inability of many modern societies to act collectively, the involvement of citizens in civil society, and their capacity for enlightened self-interest, becomes more and more significant. This is particularly true as we struggle to make difficult public choices in the resolution of complex problems such as crime, racism, poverty, and drug abuse.

Fortunately, there are communities today in which involvement in civic life is still strong. Therefore, even though much of the research in political socialization has failed to focus on citizen involvement in civil society, there are opportunities for such research. This book takes advantage of one such opportunity by exploring the socialization of citizen models in one community in the northeastern United States. To understand how and why citizens become involved in civil society, it is necessary to first define civil society and to explore its influence on citizen behavior.

Chapter 2

Civil Society

The focus of this book is the process by which citizens are socialized to be active in civil society and concerned with issues surrounding public life. This process is significant, since civil society is critical to the success of democratic institutions and to ameliorate the dysfunctional individualism that can pervade modern society. Civil society is also the space in which individuals come to theorize and to act within public life. This chapter will provide arguments for the importance of civil society to political socialization, and therefore to democratic institutions. It will also provide a historical context to more fully understand the meaning and practices of American civil society as well as contextualize the conception of civil society being applied in this book. The chapter will begin by providing a definition of and conditions necessary to civil society.

Civil society is a "contingent, indeterminate historical formation" (Perez-Diaz, 1995, p. 93) that is not necessarily guaranteed in any society but is a product of certain conditions forming within a society.

> [These conditions include the following core institutions:] a government which is limited and accountable and operates under the rule of law; a market economy (implying a regime of private property); an array of free, voluntary associations (political, economic, social, and cultural); and a sphere of free public debate. (Perez-Diaz, 1995, p. 81)

The beginnings of civil society can be traced to the removal of the central power of Rome (Hall, 1995). After that time, "state building took place within a field of preexistent social forces" (Hall, 1995, p. 4), including the church, particularly in an ideological sense, and the feudal nobility, whose rights, particularly property, had already been in practice. This dispersal of social forces, and the need for kings to bind nobility together for purposes of war, maintained the space necessary for civil society to grow. Hall states that "kings sought to enhance their powers by granting autonomy to towns; these became islands within the feudal sea in which new ideas and practices could develop" (Hall, 1995, p. 4).

Today, the creation of this space between the state and the individual is referred to as civil society, "the realm of volunteer networks and informal associations in which individuals conduct most of their lives" (Eberly, 1994, p. xxx). Existing within this space are what Berger and Neuhaus (1996) identified as mediating institutions. These institutions include families, religious organizations, voluntary associations of various kinds, and neighborhoods. All of these institutions mediate between "the individual in his private life and the large institutions of public life" (Berger & Neuhaus, 1996, p. 158). The modern state and economic conglomerates represent the large institutions of public life that Berger and Neuhaus refer to as "metastructures."

Berger's and Neuhaus's (1996) position on the importance of these mediating structures reflects that of Derber's (1996) and Putnam's (1993) position on civil society. Primarily, all of these theorists believe that civil society and the mediating institutions that make up society are the realms in which values are generated and maintained. Furthermore, civil society is the space in which meaning[1] develops for citizens, and where citizens learn communal forms of action.

Those who believe that civil society teaches or promotes civic activity are referred to as "civil society theorists" (Kymlicka & Norman, 1997).

> These theorists emphasize the necessity of civility and self-restraint to a healthy democracy but deny that either the market or political participation is sufficient to teach these virtues. Instead, it is in the voluntary organizations of civil society—churches, families, unions, ethnic associations, cooperatives, environmental groups, neighborhood associations, women's support groups, charities—that we learn the virtues of mutual obligation. (Kymlicka & Norman, 1997, p. 12)

While this book is partly concerned with the socialization patterns within civil society, it is primarily interested in other explanations for individual engagement in civil society, particularly the involvement in voluntary associations.[2] Civil society theorists focus on the socializing effects of civil society. This research takes on a similar focus but examines patterns of socialization that first lead to involvement in civil society.

A critique of civil society theorists argues that there is little, if any, empirical evidence that involvement in civil society and in mediating institutions does lead to further social involvement and to enlightened self-interest. Debates over the significance of civil society are mostly theoretical, with little research to support the various claims. And while there is historical evidence that provides some support for the influence of civil society on enlightened self-interest, this evidence does not examine how individuals conceptualize the world, concepts that direct personal action (Ferguson, 1971; Boyte, 1989; Hall, 1995).

Historical evidence suggests that some of the mediating institutions of civil society do not necessarily teach democratic values and practices. These institutions or organizations (i.e., white supremacist organizations, some right to life groups, Ku Klux Klan, etc.) may support male dominance over woman, deference to religious authority, and intolerance of other faiths and races (Kymlicka & Norman, 1997). Walzer refers to this as "critical associationalism" and suggests that some associations might need to be reformed in light of the principles of democratic citizenship (i.e., tolerance, justice, equality) (as cited in Kymlicka & Norman, 1997, p. 13).

The fact that civic networks and associations can be both negative and positive when it comes to teaching citizenship, particularly citizenship that reflects enlightened self-interest and tolerance, creates a tension that Berger and Neuhaus (1996) view as significant to continuing problems such as racism in the United States. They suggest that public policy needs to be proscriptive and not prescriptive with regard to civil society and these mediating institutions. Public policy has to encourage and enforce civil rights, but it should not overly legislate the determination of mediating structures.

In examining civil society, further distinctions must be made. While civil society is connected to the public sector or the state, it is a "voluntary, 'private' realm devoted to 'public' goods" and can make "no claim to exercise monopoly on legitimate coercion" (Barber, 1995, p. 114). Also important to note is that the public sector, which is related to the state, is coordinated by power, while the private sector, related to the market, is coordinated by money (Cohen, 1995). Cohen (1995) also argues that there is another structure—political society—that mediates between civil society and the state. Her view of political society and the state is the focus of most research in political socialization. Generally, research on political society involves the role of citizen involvement in the formation of political parties, lobbies, and other bargaining forums that directly influence the state.

While this book is not primarily interested in Cohen's *political society* or the direct influence of citizen action on the state, it recognizes that local governments are often part of the network of individuals within communities, networks that allow for informal as well as formal solutions to local concerns. These local mechanisms of the state stand just outside of the primary groups[3] in which we spend the majority of our lives. The representatives of local governments usually maintain loyalties to the community rather than to the state, thus they are more interested in the community than in the possibility of enhancing their own political aspirations.

Another aspect of this research that Barber (1995, p. 115) notes is that individuals who participate in civil society do not recognize it as political action; they do not realize the significance of their activities within a larger political context. As will be shown in chapter 6, many of the subjects included in this study would find it insulting to conceptualize their participation in civil society as political. Barber (1995) suggests, however, that we need to be aware of the importance of how we name the mediating institutions of civil society. He also suggests that the failure to recognize labor unions and environmental organizations as part of civil society, and instead as serving private interests, has led to their being referred to or identified as "special interest groups."

The very notion of what is *political* is also confusing. At a fundamental level, politics is about the mutual benefits of social organizations and the decision-making processes that determine those organizations (Hummel, 1980). Certainly it becomes clear in this book that the associational networks in which people place themselves have been helpful in times of need. These networks could be used for an informal exchange or even to influence local officials. On the other hand, the distinction that Cohen (1995) makes is useful, since she provides another layer, *political society*, between civil society and the state. Both power and the processes for continued political conflict are developed in political society.

While not all voluntary associations would claim to be political, it is clear that associations within civil society are often political. In this research, even religious organizations were discovered to be networks where individuals could gain access to decision makers within the community. One of the subjects in this study, Jan Hyland, said that she is able to access individuals in church "who are very connected in the town." These individuals know how to get things done and who to call to resolve problems within the town. Participation in these "non-political" associations also provides contacts for joining more politically oriented groups, as well as teaching the necessary skills to be effective in such political organizations, according to Verba, Schlozman, and Brady (1995).

IMPORTANCE OF CIVIL SOCIETY TO DEMOCRACY

The significance of civil society to democratic institutions is presented in both Derber's book, *The Wilding of America: How Greed and Violence Are Eroding Our Nation's Character* (1996), and Putnam's text, *Making Democracy Work: Civic Traditions in Modern Italy* (1993). Derber argues that civil society is essential to fortify America's character against *wilding*, a degenerate form of individualism (1996, p. 2). He argues that modern society has a declining ability to socialize citizens toward more collective concerns for public life, and that those institutions, particularly the market, that have been successful are socializing people to become more isolated and concerned with their own self-interest, thus lacking any public context.

In Putnam's book, we learn how specific civic attributes or variables reinforce local or regional governments within a democratic system. These variables include the "vibrancy of associational life," local media or newspaper readership, referenda voting, and preference voting (Putnam, 1993, pp. 91–94). While not all of these variables are significant to the findings of this study, many of Putnam's other concepts, including norms of general reciprocity (p. 171), are significant to the subjects' descriptions of their lives and their communities. Furthermore, Putnam's position on the significance of civil society to democratic institutions provides context for the importance of this type of research.

Putnam maintains that participation in civil society is at the heart of democratic political life (1993). He studied the regional governance system instituted in Italy in 1970 and asked, "*what are the conditions for creating strong, effective representative institutions*" (p. 6, emphasis in original). He was first interested in how social institutions shaped politics, and how these institutions were shaped by history. The criteria he used for defining successful democratic institutions were their abilities to move citizens toward the resolution of political differences in a responsive and an effective manner.

Putnam chose the four indicators of the "civic-ness of regional life" (1993, pp. 91–94) mentioned earlier. Two of these indicators reflect de Tocqueville's "broad conception of what we have termed the civic community" (Putnam, 1993, p. 91), and two directly reflect political behavior. The indicators that reflect de Tocqueville's civic community include "vibrancy of associational life" (Putnam, 1993, p. 91) and the connection between associational life and local media or newspaper readership. The indicators of political behavior were referenda turnout and preference voting. Putnam suggests that referenda turnout reflects "a politics of issues," while preference voting reflects "the politics of patronage" (1993, p. 95). He elucidates the distinctiveness of these two political acts:

> Political behavior in some regions presumes that politics is about collective deliberation on public issues. By contrast, politics elsewhere is organized hierarchically and focused more narrowly on personal advantage. (1993, p. 96)

Putnam (1993) finds that these indicators, combined into a single *Civic Community Index*, show a "remarkable concordance between the performance of a regional government and the degree to which social and political life in that region approximates the ideal of a civic community" (p. 98).

Putnam (1993) argues that in communities that had a low Civic Community Index, individuals felt "exploited, alienated, powerless" (p. 109). Power was organized around a hierarchy that promoted the centralization of authority and increased citizen dependency on this hierarchy for patronage. This hierarchy also tended to be represented by an elite from the most "privileged portion of the population" (p. 101).

In contrast, communities that scored high on the Civic Community Index were more supportive of political equality. The citizens in these communities were more likely to vote for egalitarian electoral reform and to dislike hierarchical authority structures (Putnam, 1993, pp. 102–104). The citizens emphasized direct engagement in the resolution of political matters.

Their concern for direct engagement is particularly significant in light of the power structure in the United States. One can make a strong argument that the United States has become more hierarchical and less responsive to direct civic participation. In the 1950s, Mills pointed out that the role of the federal government has grown at the same time that it has also become more and more influenced by a "capitalist elite" or the "corporate class" (Mills, 1956; see also Dye, 1995). The elite's main influence is to determine the political agenda. This is done, to some extent, by controlling the enormous amount of funding necessary to run for politic office.

Corporations have become the main source for political campaign financing in the United States. The *Washington Post* (September 20, 1990) reported that 70 percent of each major party's contributions now comes from corporations. This money is influential because of the high cost of elections. Senate campaigns now require a minimum of $3 million per candidate. A House seat can cost over $250,000, and in a fairly recent election for the California's gubernatorial race, the Democratic and Republican candidates each spent in excess of $40 million (CNN News, November 8, 1994). With this amount of campaign spending becoming a necessity, politicians look to those who have vast resources, primarily corporations. This corporate influence can be even stronger in state governments, where funds can have a greater impact and where politicians are more closely tied to local companies.

Greider (1992) points out that the "most pernicious effect of campaign money is probably not on the legislative roll calls, but in how money works to keep important new ideas off the table—ideas that might find a popular constituency among citizens, but would offend important contributors" (p. 259). In addition, corporations spend over $941 million to promote their images through broadcasting and print. This amount is enough to finance four out of five presidential campaigns (Greider, 1992, p. 339).

Another growing problem in the United States has to do with dilemmas of collective action (see note 2, chapter 1, for descriptions of dilemmas of collective action) that involve the inability of individuals to cooperate for mutual benefit. This is ironic, since Hummel (1980) suggests that social organization is the basis of political association and economic well-being. However, as Putnam (1993) points out, there are several instances, including the tragedy of the commons, public goods, logic of collective action, and the prisoner's dilemma, in which refusal to cooperate may seem to be the rational choice, even though, in fact, it may not be. In each of these dilemmas, Putnam (1993) suggests that if "actors are unable to make credible commitments to one another, they must forgo many opportunities for mutual gain" (p. 164). The ability to make these credible commitments has to do with "social capital" or "features of social organization, such as trust, norms, and networks, that can improve the efficiency of society by facilitating coordinated actions" (Putnam, 1993, p. 167). The only other alternative is third-party enforcement, which is coercive and, as such, expensive.

Putnam argues that social capital is an expansive good that develops historically and grows with use. The sources of social capital are built up through the personal relations and networks of private life (i.e., "I know I can trust that person to work on my house, because I know his wife's family."). He suggests that social trust develops from norms of reciprocity and networks of civic engagement.

Norms of reciprocity are of two sorts, "balanced (or 'specific') and 'general' (or 'diffuse')" (Putnam, 1993, p. 172).

> Balanced reciprocity refers to a simultaneous exchange of items of equivalent value, as when office-mates exchange holiday gifts or legislators log-roll. Generalized reciprocity refers to a continuing relationship of exchange that is at any given time unrequited or imbalanced, but that involves mutual expectations that a benefit granted now should be repaid in the future. (Putnam, 1993, p. 172)

Generalized reciprocity helps develop social trust. Such trust must be advanced within a specific context of personal relations in which it will be "requited, not exploited" over a period of time (Putnam, 1993, p. 172). Numerous examples of the subjects studied in this research reflect practices of general reciprocity in their lives, such as neighbors helping to clear fallen trees after a storm or helping to finish building a widow's house.

Putnam's (1993) basic argument is that civic communities lead to and are a product of social capital. This capital resolves dilemmas of collective action and allows for the successful development of democratic institutions. These institutions then encourage attitudes and behaviors that lead to furthering social capital.

Putnam's work (1993) suggests that civil society is important to democratic government, from two perspectives. First, in communities where strong associational networks exist, one is more likely to find citizens who are engaged in political issues that are important to their immediate needs; more importantly, they are also invested in issues that impact on public life. This participation in public life by larger numbers of citizens creates a more egalitarian political structure and serves to balance the power of government officials with the power of the citizenry. The second perspective is that civil society helps develop the social capital to resolve problems of collective action without the costly use of force or coercion.

Charles Derber (1996) sees civil society as the answer to *wilding*, a degenerative form of individualism that has grown in the United States. Derber (1996) suggests that there are two forms of wilding. The first is expressive wilding, which is behind actions designed for "the sheer satisfaction of indulging one's own destructive impulses" (p. 6). The second, which is the focus of his study, is instrumental wilding. This refers to the attainment of money, career advancement, or other personal gain in spite of the harm it can cause others. He suggests that the determination of wilding depends on an individual's motivation, empathy, and the level of harm inflicted on another (p. 10), and says that instrumental wilding can take an economic, a political, or a social form.

> *Economic wilding* is the morally uninhibited pursuit of money by individuals or businesses at the expense of others. *Political wilding* is the abuse of political office to benefit oneself or one's own social class, or the wielding of political authority to inflict morally unacceptable sufferings on citizens at home or abroad. *Social wilding* ranges from personal or family acts of violence, such as child or spouse abuse, to collective forms of selfishness that weaken society, such as affluent suburbs turning their backs on bleeding central cities. (Derber, 1996, p. 8)

He also suggests that there can be individualistic and communal forms of wilding, and that the former is "more predominant in the United States" (Derber, 1996, p. 10). Derber believes that the individualistic type of wilding in the United States reflects a history of a competitive free market and a culture of individualism.

Drawing from both Marx and Durkheim, Derber sees the roots of this individualism in the political socialization practices that have evolved in the United States. First of all, Derber reflects on Durkheim's concern over the weakening of social solidarity in the modern societies. Durkheim saw the bonds that unite the individual to the rest of society being "slackened or broken" (Durkheim, as cited in Derber, 1996, p. 15). Without these ties to society, an individual who "finds no meaning in genuine collective activity" (ibid.) is, according to Derber, "primed for wilding" (Derber, 1996, p. 15).

Derber (1996) suggests that the socialization or, better yet, the undersocialization of individuals to collective activity "reflects a weakened community less able to regulate its increasingly individualistic members" (p. 16). These patterns of socialization are reflective of a society whose institutions no longer carry the authority necessary to instill social values into future generations. He states that the breakdown of community and the failure of social institutions to properly socialize citizens lead to a sociopathic society in which there is a collapse of moral order.

At the other end of the spectrum of socialization is the society that over-socializes individuals around the meaning of collective will. Such patterns of socialization can be counterproductive to liberal ideals of the good society. Derber (1996) considers this problem in light of Marx's argument that capitalism can manipulate and reproduce value systems that emphasize only competition and profit seeking. Derber sees this oversocialization in the context of the American Dream of material success, a dream perpetuated by capitalism.

> American wilding is a form of socially prescribed antisocial behavior, modeled by leaders and reinforced by the rules of our free market game. As such, it re-flects less the insufficient presence of society in individuals than overconfor-mity to a society whose norms and values are socially dangerous. (Derber, 1996, p. 16)

The growth of these socially dangerous values has weakened local communities, as Durkheim suggests, and is due to the centralization of control over the media.

> As local communities weaken, giant corporations, including the media, ad-vertising, and communications industries, shape the appetites, morality, and behavior of Americans ever more powerfully. (Derber, 1996, p. 17)

The growth of media influence, particularly television, also has occurred during a period during which Ronald Reagan, George Bush, and Newt Gin-grich have dominated the political landscape. Ronald Reagan's political phi-losophy is based on the idea that the market will direct the "selfish energies of the entrepreneur into socially productive channels" (Derber, 1996, p. 40). Un-fortunately, Reagan designed the economic rules to favor the established eco-nomic elite, who continued to accumulate wealth during a time where there was an ever-widening gap between rich and poor (Phillips, 1990). According to sociologist Robert Merton, the effect of disparity of wealth leads a society, whose wants and expectations far outdistance real opportunities to meet those expectations, toward criminal activity (as cited in Derber, 1996, p. 17).

Global capitalism is another influence on the market. As multinational corporations begin to lose their ties to nations, the laws and values of any na-tion no longer obligate them. Traditional organizations and structures, such as unions and governmental agencies, which have stopped the abuses of manage-ment on labor, can no longer influence these corporations. Without any rules, these organizations have no restrictions on where greed can take them, and thus they easily resort to economic wilding. Multinational corporations also no longer rely on domestic labor. They can easily neglect the poor of any nation as long as surplus labor is available elsewhere (Derber, 1996).

The outcomes of these influences have led to pure self-interest at the expense of empathy and moral sensibility, according to Kanter and Mirvis (as cited in Derber, 1996). In their survey, Kanter and Mirvis found that close to half of the U.S. population holds the basic assumption "that most people are only out for themselves, and that you are better off zapping them before they do it to you" (Kanter & Mirvis, as cited in Derber, 1996, p. 90).

The results of these patterns of socialization have had an impact on all classes in the United States. Derber cites Philippe Bourgois, who conducted a study on drug dealers in East Harlem. He quotes Bourgois:

> [The view that] the poor have been badly socialized and do not share mainstream values is wrong. On the contrary, ambitious, energetic inner-city youth are attracted to the underground [drug dealing] economy precisely because they believe in the rags-to-riches American Dream. Like many in the mainstream, they are frantically trying to get their piece of the pie as fast as possible. (Bourgois, as cited in Derber, 1996, p. 97)

The impact on wealthier classes also has been noted, particularly within an educational context. Derber (1996, p. 92) points to a report of the Carnegie Foundation for Advancement of Teaching, released in 1990, which found "a breakdown of civility and other disruptive forces" that leave campuses "in tatters" (Fiske, as cited in Derber, 1996, p. 92). The report points out that many students have little interest in their studies and are concerned more for what an education means in terms of high-paying jobs.

Derber (1996) argues that part of the problem may be due to the socialization that occurs in the family. He suggests that higher income parents provide their children with money rather than attention in order to pursue their own professional careers. These same parents, often living in suburbia, are, in fact, causing violence to their children through these patterns of neglect (1996, p. 113). Jean Bethke Elshtain (1995) makes a similar argument. She says that the "democratic dispositions" (p. 2) necessary for public life are not being taught in the family. She suggests that parenting today requires a greater commitment from civil society to help stabilize family life.

This breakdown in family life is a pattern of the "breakdown in both the physical and social infrastructure necessary to keep a society together" (Derber, 1996, p. 115). While money continues to feed the Pentagon, little is finding its way to support the poor or to support the public spaces and facilities necessary for social and economic success (Derber, 1996, p. 116). Derber (1996, p. 127) argues that a triage of sorts is occurring in the poor neighborhoods of our cities. These neighborhoods are cut off from support from outlying areas or public sources. The only control left for these areas are prisons and police.

While they do not offer suggestions on how to encourage direct involvement in civil society, both Derber and Elshtain believe that civil society is the space in which individuals can move beyond self-interest to enlightened self-interest, a perspective that cannot be forced onto individuals by the state. This lack of force is a significant point in understanding the voluntary nature of civil society and the limitations of the state in this arena. As Derber (1996) points out, civil society cannot be coerced, but it "must arise from the cooperation and moral sensibilities of ordinary people who understand that their own fulfillment requires thriving communities and an intact society" (p. 145).

This is not to say that the state cannot promote civil society through the structuring of social and political institutions. Civil society "blooms only where markets and governments are kept in reasonable check, and families, communities, and voluntary associations, the institutional seedbeds of love, morality, and trust, are free to prosper" (Derber, 1996, p. 146). To accomplish this, the state must realize that it "cannot raise and socialize children, but one of its highest priorities should be to help finance and save the institutions, including the family and schools, that can do the job" (Derber, 1996, p. 160).

Finally, Derber (1996) argues that wilding can only be cured when individuals take responsibility for their lives and the lives of others. He believes that individuals must participate in civil society where the creation of sustained social movements can help the fight against greedy multinational corporations and unresponsive governments. The structure of our society must begin to focus not only on the market and the economic conditions but also on the social conditions that allow such markets to persist.

HISTORY OF CIVIL SOCIETY IN AMERICA

The importance of civil society is best understood within a historical context. The founding of the American colonies and their progression toward a democratic state was unique in the history of Western states. Fortunately, this history and the significance of civil society was well documented by Alexis de Tocqueville (1848/1990). His writings evidence some of the earlier practices and attitudes that developed around public problem solving. Traces of these practices and citizen perspectives on the role of politics and the state are still present in contemporary American society, as evidenced in this research.

De Tocqueville (1848/1990) observed civil society in the early stages of the American Republic. He observed a differentiation between the associations that make up civil society. Political associations focused on the issues and uses of state power, and civil associations focused on more local and immediate issues. De Tocqueville observed three degrees of political association. The first degree of political association "channels the efforts of divergent minds and urges them vigorously toward the one end. . . . The second degree in the exercise of the right of association is the power of meeting," and the third degree of political association is "the partisans of an opinion may unite in electoral bodies and choose delegates to represent them in a central assembly" (de Tocqueville, 1848/1990, vol. 1, p. 192).

As he did in much of his work, de Tocqueville (1848/1990) contrasts the associations in the United States with those in Europe. In the United States, these associations served to show numerical strength and diminish the moral power of the majority, to stimulate competition of ideas, and, lastly, to "entertain hopes of drawing over the majority to their own side" (de Tocqueville, 1848/1990, vol. 1, p. 196). In Europe, these associations could not expect to draw other citizens to their side because of the diverse political perspectives of the citizenry. Therefore, these European associations fought against the state and those associations that had some control of it. The contrast was due to the fact that "the differences of opinion [in the United States] are mere differences of hue" (de Tocqueville, 1848/1990, vol. 1, p. 197).

Although differences existed among associations in the United States, de Tocqueville pointed out that they are intricately linked. "Civil associations, therefore, facilitate political association; but, on the other hand, political association singularly strengthens and improves associations for civil purposes" (de Toqueville, 1848/1990, vol. 2, p. 115). The relationship, he suggests, is twofold. Similar to Verba, Schlozman, and Brady (1995), de Tocqueville finds that small affairs in the community help individuals pursue larger political goals in common. "The greater the multiplicity of small affairs, the more do men, even without knowing it, acquire facility in prosecuting great undertakings in common" (de Tocqueville, 1848/1990, vol., 2, p. 115). On the other hand, he suggests that there is what we would call today a "cost-benefit factor" regarding work in smaller causes. He suggests that if citizens did not see the value of association in the larger causes, then they may not see their interest in attending to smaller causes. "In politics men combine for great undertakings, and the use they make of the principle of association in important affairs practically teaches them that it is their interest to help one another in those of less moment" (de Tocqueville, 1848/1990, vol. 2, p. 116).

The growth of both of these types of associations was unique to the Americas, according to de Tocqueville. While the principle of association was part of the social life brought over from England and was always a part of American society, the growth and the habit of the Americans in forming these associations was notable. De Tocqueville was first struck by the multitude of associations.

In no country in the world has the principal of association been more successfully used or applied to a greater multitude of objects than in America. Besides the permanent associations which are established by law under the names of townships, cities, and counties, a vast number of others are formed and maintained by the agency of private individuals. (de Tocqueville, 1848/1990, vol. 1, p. 191)

The Americans seemed to value the self-reliance afforded by these associations, and de Tocqueville remarked how even children were well socialized around this value as revealed in their play. This is particularly interesting in its contrast to the remarks made by the subjects in this book on the contemporary development of children's play and its control by adults.

The citizen of the United States is taught from infancy to rely upon his own exertions in order to resist the evils and the difficulties of life; he looks upon the social authority with an eye of mistrust and anxiety, and he claims its assistance only when he is unable to do without it. This habit may be traced even in the schools, where the children in their games are wont to submit to rules which they have themselves established, and to punish misdemeanors which they have themselves defined. (de Tocqueville, 1848/1990, vol. 1, p. 191)

Lastly, these associations were able to resolve problems of collective life, a circumstance that was rarely effective in Europe.

The same spirit pervades every act of social life. If a stoppage occurs in a thoroughfare and the circulation of vehicles is hindered, the neighbors immediately form themselves into a deliberative body; and this extemporaneous assembly gives rise to an executive power which remedies the inconvenience before anybody has thought of recurring to a pre-existing authority superior to that of the persons immediately concerned. If some public pleasure is concerned, an association is formed to give more splendor and regularity to the entertainment. Societies are formed to resist evils that are exclusively of a moral nature, as to diminish the vice of intemperance. In the United States associations are established to promote the public safety, commerce, industry, morality, and religion. There is no end which the human will despairs of attaining through the combined power of individuals united into a society. (de Tocqueville, 1848/1990, vol. 1, pp. 191–192)

De Tocqueville believed that these associations were effective in America because they were necessary. While in France problems may be resolved by the government, and in England they may be resolved by a person of rank, in the United States, "you will be sure to find an association" (vol. 2, p. 106). In a sense, conditions of equality required Americans to rely on and combine efforts to make use of their resources; in Europe, resources were already centralized within an aristocratic order. The unique condition of equality in America did have some negative consequences, however, particularly on the growth of individualism.

Not only did de Tocqueville foresee the growth of individualism in America, but he also saw civil society's ability to balance some of the negative consequences of this individualism. He described individualism as "a mature and calm feeling, which disposes each member of the community to sever himself from the mass of his fellows and to draw apart with his family and his friends, so that after he has thus formed a little circle of his own, he willingly leaves society at large to itself" (de Tocqueville, 1848/1990, vol. 2, p. 98).

The economic and social equality of the United States, relative to Europe, created the conditions for the origins of individualism. De Tocqueville said that "... individualism is of democratic origin, and it threatens to spread in the same ratio as the equality of condition" (de Tocqueville, 1848/1990, vol. 2, p. 98). In Europe, the aristocracy made "a chain of all the members of the community, from the peasant to the king; democracy breaks that chain and severs every link of it" (de Tocqueville, 1848/1990, vol. 2, p. 99). He suggested that as social conditions become more equal, more people have enough on their own to "owe nothing to any man" (ibid.). They saw themselves as "standing alone" and were "apt to imagine that their whole destiny is in their own hands" (ibid.).

According to de Tocqueville, civil society balanced this tendency toward individualism. He said that Americans "have combated by free institutions the tendency of equality to keep men asunder, and they have subdued it" (de Tocqueville, 1848/1990, vol. 2, p. 103). Through engagement in local affairs, citizens became acquainted and learned to rely on one another, to trust one another, and to listen to one another.

> Thus far more may be done by entrusting to the citizens the administration of minor affairs than by surrendering to them in the control of important ones, towards interesting them in the public welfare and convincing them that they constantly stand in need of one another in order to provide for it. (de Tocqueville, 1848/1990, vol. 2, p. 104)

De Tocqueville also suggested that this engagement in local affairs had a moral dimension. Associational life led to a common understanding of one's duty and enabled the individual to move beyond the simple position of self-interest to the concept of enlightened self-interest, mentioned earlier.

> The free institutions which the inhabitants of the United States possess, and the political rights of which they make so much use, remind every citizen, and in a thousand ways, that he lives in society. They every instant impress upon his mind the notion that it is the duty as well as the interest of men to make themselves useful to their fellow creatures; and as he sees no particular ground

of animosity to them, since he is never either their master or their slave, his heart readily leans to the side of kindness. Men attend to the interests of the public, first by necessity, afterwards by choice; what was intentional becomes an instinct, and by dint of working for the good of one's fellow citizens, the habit and the taste for serving them are at length acquired. (de Tocqueville, 1848/1990, vol. 2, p. 105)

The American moralists do not profess that men ought to sacrifice themselves for their fellow creatures *because* it is noble to make such sacrifices, but they boldly aver that such sacrifices are as necessary to him who imposes them upon himself as to him for whose sake they are made. (de Tocqueville, 1848/1990, vol. 2, p. 121, emphasis in original)

The experience of serving the public good taught the value of service to mankind as a moral lesson, a lesson that promoted broader notions of self-interest. Enlightened self-interest was a concept that was particularly practical and tangible in American society. It was not a lofty concept of the exceptionally virtuous citizen but reflected the everyday actions of much of the population. "The principle of self-interest rightly understood produces no great acts of self-sacrifice, but it suggests daily small acts of self-denial" (de Tocqueville, 1848/1990, vol. 2, p. 123).

De Tocqueville also saw the growing need, however, to teach the support of this concept. He was likely seeing individualism begin to increase in social significance and anticipated the need to balance individualism with structured socialization experiences that would promote collective action.

Educate, then, at any rate, for the age of implicit self-sacrifice and instinctive virtues is already flitting far away from us, and the time is fast approaching when freedom, public peace, and social order itself will not be able to exist without education. (de Tocqueville, 1848/1990, vol. 2, p. 124)

Even within this model, self-interest rightly understood, it is necessary not only to construct society around these reinforcing experiences but also to teach the habits of the mind that will support the understanding of this principle.

Today, there is a decline in civil society (Barber, 1995; Boyte, 1989). Barber (1995) suggests that after the Civil War, industrial growth and the market began to "encroach on and crush civil society" (p. 116). In response to some of the negative impacts on this growth, the government began to intervene in the market, and without grassroots public participation, it too began to squeeze out civil society. Barber (1995) suggests that sometime "between the two Roosevelts, it vanished altogether" (p. 116).

Boyte (1989) says that Franklin Delano Roosevelt "borrowed his understanding of politics and government largely from Herbert Croly . . . who explicitly redefined 'democracy' away from any local, civic activity to what he called the 'great community' of the state" (p. 42). This perspective and that of Walter Lippmann offer that with the growth of the modern state, communal associations were no longer viable, and that political life would be absorbed into the modern forms of communication available to us as a nation. This perspective led to the notion that citizen participation in the day-to-day affairs of governance could be better performed by a modern bureaucratic state. While there were arguments made at the time that the organization of citizens was critical, the "reins of power in the construction of twentieth-century reform have been held by self-described liberals who had little use for an active, independent citizenry" (Boyte, 1989, p. 43).

The emphasis of the state in securing liberties challenged by the growth of industrial capitalism downplayed the citizen's role (Boyte, 1989). In fact, there was a growing belief in the ability of a technical bureaucracy to solve any and all problems of a public nature. This reliance on bureaucracy served to erode the very notion of public space. "In a world where citizens no longer meet, the concept of 'public' becomes increasingly thin and specialized—the preserve of representatives, guided by experts and professionals" (Boyte, 1989, p. 42).

These experts and professionals set out to solve all of the problems within a value-free, decision-making environment. Social sciences were modeled on the natural sciences, with the belief that value-free social science would be as valid and reliable as natural science; the application of social science research would determine politically neutral solutions to problems of public policy.

Positioning the state in conflict with large-scale capitalist institutions eroded the populist associations of the 1930s, 1940s, and 1950s (Boyte, 1989). These associations were outgrowths of popular movements, including those of freed slaves, women's rights, farmers, and the urban working class. Boyte (1989) states that the basic problem "in renewing citizen politics has been the question of how people can regain sufficient power and confidence to make strong citizenship a serious possibility" (p. 48). Boyte (1989) reviews the 1950s' work of Saul Alinsky, remarking that while a "number of democratic theorists in America—from Walter Rauschenbusch, Jane Adams, and John Dewey to Martin Luther King Jr.—have addressed the problem, none has done so with more skill and thoroughness than the late Saul Alinsky" (p. 48).

Alinsky's mark on social movements was his emphasis on how to develop the organization and resources necessary to have power (Boyte, 1989). This was particularly necessary for the poor, who had to deal with a bureaucracy that tended to impose solutions rather than work with the communities they were designed to support (Boyte, 1989).

The success of popular action in the late twentieth century was based around the practices of community orientation (Boyte, 1989). It was in examining the unique aspects and networks of communities that theorists such as

Saul Alinsky found success. Unfortunately, Alinsky lacked a "visionary dimension" on which to base his work and the organization of social movements of the time (Boyte, 1989, p. 61). In essence, there were no practices of realizing common ends, and such organizations came increasingly to focus on particular self-interests (Boyte, 1989). By the time President Reagan came into office, with his emphasis on the marketplace as the space to resolve public problems, the whole dimension of public life, particularly civil society, had collapsed (Boyte, 1989).

THE CREATION OF MEANING AND CIVIL SOCIETY

Interest in civil society in the modern state is beginning to gain more attention. This attention comes from a variety of political perspectives, and these various perspectives provide differing descriptions for how the mediating institutions of civil society should be constructed as well as the role of the state in regard to individual liberty. Populist and communitarian perspectives are more relevant to this book, particularly because these perspectives focus on community life and on the primary groups that are more likely to influence the individual.

The variety of perspectives with which one can view the place of civil society in the United States includes traditionalist, libertarian, populist, and communitarian (Eberly, 1994). The traditionalist views civil society as being comprised of a hierarchy of mediating institutions that rely on each other, including marriage, household, community, state, nation, and corporation. Marriage is considered "the first and most natural social bond" (Carlson, 1994, p. 293) and is the basis upon which all other social bonds and related institutions rely. Marriage is seen as a "covenant between the couple and their kin" and as a "covenant between the couple and the broader community" (Carlson, 1994, pp. 294–295).

The second "natural bond" is the household (Carlson, 1994, pp. 294–295). This is the bond upon which all political life is based. These households must have "the power to shelter, feed, and clothe their members in the absence of both state and corporate largesse" (Carlson, 1994, pp. 295–296). For the household to provide for itself, it must be connected to the land.[4] This perspective also suggests that this connection provides for a "natural wisdom unobtainable in any other way" (Carlson, 1994, p. 297). The household must be self-sufficient and have control over the means of production. Within the household, there must be an authority structure where "all family members defer to the wisdom of elders, where children defer to the guidance of parents, and where wives defer to the public authority of husbands" (Carlson, 1994, p. 298). The household then mediates the relations and connections to other loyalties such as state, nation, ideology, or corporation.

The third social bond is the community, one's village, town, tribe, or neighborhood. These "collectives operate best when bonded by other affections: a common religious faith; a shared ethnicity; a binding sense of history; the intermingling of a relatively small number of kin groups" (Carlson, 1994, pp. 298–299). The bond suggested here is commerce. The community setting allows for exchange between households and discourages deviance through shunning, a practice that can only be done when there are close social bonds. These bonds are created, and spontaneous leadership develops through the "attachments of individuals to the landscape in which they grow, live, and act, and to the flora and fauna of their native place" (Carlson, 1994, p. 300).

The next, or fourth natural social bond, is to the state, whose role is to protect citizens from external threat and to mediate disputes between households and communities that cannot be handled locally. The dominant principle here is that the state has limited powers.

The nation is the last and broadest social bond. "It rests on commonalties that transcend households, communities, and states, among them religious belief, language, a shared history, a common ecosystem, inherited folkways, and blood" (Carlson, 1994, p. 301). The traditionalist perspective suggests that this last bond, while "necessary to a complete or full social life, is properly mediated through the foundational tiers of state, community, and household" (Carlson, 1994, p. 302).

The corporation is seen as the "wild card" with this model, and it can disrupt some of the "natural" bonds and cause social disintegration (Carlson, 1994, p. 302). There is a need for a "balance between the satisfactions of continuity through community and the disruptions spawned by corporate-driven change" (Carlson, 1994, p. 303).

While this perspective offers some insight into a building block of social bonds and meaning for individuals within nation-states, it seems wholly impractical. First of all, it values hierarchical relations that are contrary to democratic ideals and the fundamental value of individual liberty. "Wives defer to the public authority of husbands" (Carlson, 1994, p. 298) is no longer a permissible approach to policy formation or societal norms. This is not to say that deferential wives do not exist; rather, it is to say that this hierarchical relation is antithetical to mainstream values of liberty and feminism.

Secondly, the economy is much too complicated to go back to an agrarian lifestyle based on local markets. Such an ideal could only occur through strict intervention by the state, somewhat akin to the Pol Pot regime in Cambodia. This intervention would be highly contradictory to the traditionalist view to the limitations of the state.

The libertarian perspective on civic society also takes on an extremely limited view of the state. It is, like the communitarian perspective, highly critical of the growth of state power in individual lives.

America's reliance on politics as the solution to most every problem and alleged problem has turned envy into official public policy, stripped individuals and communities of their traditional social responsibilities, destroyed economic opportunities for the disadvantaged, promoted unjust foreign intervention, and undermined private moral and spiritual values. (Bandow, 1994, p. 321)

This perspective suggests that life should be organized around civil society and not the state (Bandow, 1994). Government should only be called in when private "discourse and action was not possible or would likely prove inadequate" (Bandow, 1994, p. 322). This view promotes the dissolution of governmental regulation to create jobs. It would push government out of the business of education, leaving it up to the marketplace and private initiatives to prepare young people for their roles in society. It would limit government's role in welfare programs. By shrinking governmental involvement in these matters, civil society would have the opportunity to expand and to allow individual and community activism.

The libertarian view, like most views regarding civil society, calls for the development of civic virtue (Bandow, 1994, p. 325). It suggests, however, that virtue cannot be taught by the state; the state tends to legislate behavior. If one cannot act because of state coercion, then is one truly virtuous? Families, churches, and other community organizations must take on the responsibility of promoting a virtuous citizenry.

There is some agreement in all of these perspectives, including the ones that follow, about the limited capacity and inability of the state to legislate virtue. It cannot truly develop virtue in such an approach, and the costs are overwhelming. Consider the great expense the state is taking on in order to build prisons. These are institutions that rarely create or promote personal or public virtue. We would expect that family, church life, and community organizations are best left to the teaching of virtue. However, the market (Bellah et al., 1992) has dominated many of these institutions. Even public schools, traditionally under local control, have been faced with privatization or the use of market mechanisms.

The libertarian belief in the freedom of the market to resolve all local and national problems is as unrealistic as the traditional approach. It denies the influence of the corporate world in the everyday lives of Americans; at the same time, it overemphasizes the influence of government in the everyday lives of Americans. As Bellah et al. (1992) (see also Barber, 1995) point out, the diminution of civil society has been a result of both the growth of government in community life and the growth of corporate influence. State action is necessary to balance the corporate domination of private lives while still maintaining a limited role in the private sector.

The next perspective provides for a limited role of government and a historically effective response to corporate largesse. The populist perspective considers citizenship as public work and public freedom. Boyte (1994) suggests that this perspective cannot only respond to the local valuation of participatory public problem solving but also promotes public problem solving at a national level. He critiques the communitarian perspective, the last perspective presented here, as pulling in opposite directions—that of local and national emphasis. National problems cannot be resolved by the concept of community. Larger problems call for groups working together that would not immediately share perspectives on justice and history. The moral language of the communitarians cannot apply to larger social problems in a diverse and complex society. Boyte (1994) argues that through much of the community organizing work that was begun by Saul Alinsky and others over the last few decades, there has been a realization that "when groups with different views on issues like affirmative action, gay rights, or abortion find ways to work together on issues like housing or teen pregnancy, the experience can improve relationships, and also lesson moral polarization" (Boyte, 1994, p. 349). Boyte stresses that there must be a promotion of citizenship as public work. It must not only be practiced within local communities but within broader concepts of public life in which there is a more diverse membership.

The last perspective that has been a reaction to liberalism and its practice in the modern era is the communitarian perspective. The three principal themes of the communitarian perspective include the "need to start a 'multilog' about responsibility" (Conner, 1994, p. 312) or a national debate about responsibility; a strengthening of community institutions as problem solvers; and striking a balance between individual rights and community responsibility (Conner, 1994). This perspective is a response to the collapse of social order within the United States and the continuing decline of citizens to take on responsibility for themselves and for others. Furthermore, there is a growing inability of self-restraint, as evidenced in Derber (1996). People see themselves as isolated individuals fighting for "me" and for "me now." This limited notion of citizenship and social order cannot maintain itself for long (Galston, 1991; Macedo, 1990). While communitarians do not reject the pursuit of individual goals, such pursuits must be balanced with the realization that long-term individual gain is maximized only within a social order. Therefore, self-interest, or what Tussman refers to as "enlightened self-interest" (Tussman, 1997), must be properly understood within a social context. The evidence of this enlightened self-interest would be what Walzer (1992, p. 92) describes as a devotion to public causes and the amount of interest in public issues.

The underlying purpose of this book is to explore the development of the notion of enlightened self-interest and its expression in community life. It is important to note that community life is the beginning point from which any understanding of social practices makes sense. This perspective articulates the communitarian perspective on civil society and reflects Hegel's notion of human reason. He suggests that human reason relies on the interaction and meaning developed by two individuals (Hegel, as cited in Daly, 1994, p. 36).

Boyte's (1994) position of populism is also relevant to the positions taken by subjects in this research, but only in a larger public context. Even Boyte argues that public behavior begins in more local forms of social life (1994, p. 339). It is within these local forms, these mediating institutions, that the skills and practices of participatory democracy begin and flourish. From there, citizens can extend to other more regional, national, or even global concerns. This study is more of a microsociological approach to the origins of civil society (Sanderson, 1995). Interests include the early stages of participation in civil society and engagement at a local level. While larger social interests may draw people into public life, as de Tocqueville suggested, the everyday interests of most Americans are concerned with local issues. Furthermore, as many of these perspectives on civil society suggest, local involvement in mediating institutions is the basis on which all other involvement takes place. Local participation in community life begins to make the democratic experience meaningful and enhances the possibility for the sustainability of larger democratic institutions concerned with the public fate.

The experience of citizens within civil society, particularly within voluntary associations dedicated to the welfare of the community, creates or—at the very least—enhances the capacity of enlightened self-interest. As Derber (1996) and Putnam (1993) point out, this capacity serves, in turn, to mediate degenerative forms of individualism and to create the social capital necessary for collective action. The ability of citizens to act for the larger common good is also becoming increasingly more important to the balance of power between the political elite and the vast majority of citizens. The current electoral system tends to promote the influence of the elite due to the costs associated with political campaigns. The attainment of political office requires candidates to raise large sums of money, leaving potential officeholders dependent on those who can contribute such funds rather than their constituents. Fund-raising continues to be an important prerequisite to remain in public office and to the attainment of more powerful positions within Congress. Consequently, it becomes necessary to promote civic engagement in a democratic society and to recognize how and why citizens choose to be involved in public life. This leads to an examination of how political socialization affects citizenship within our society.

Chapter 3

Engaging Citizens in Civil Society

Given the importance of civil society to broadening self-interest, encouraging the possibility of collective action, and tempering the influence of excessive individualism in the United States, we need to be more conscious of the ways in which various social institutions—family, school, church, community organizations, and so on—increase the likelihood of citizen involvement in civil society. This requires an understanding of why people become involved in the various voluntary associations that make up civil society, and how their life histories lead to such involvement.

Unfortunately, research into this area is limited. Typically, researchers have been more occupied with political society—the mediating structures between civil society and the state (Cohen, 1995). Interest in political society focuses on attitudes and behaviors related to voting patterns rather than understanding involvement in voluntary associations that are not directly related to public policy. However, the research on citizen involvement in public policy is important to examine, as there is a fine line between political society and its organizations and the community voluntary associations of civil society. Verba, Schlozman, and Brady (1995) point out that these latter associations often teach the skills and provide the networks that lead to activity in political society.

Two major works in understanding involvement in both voluntary associations and political society are *Voice and Equality: Civic Voluntarism in American Politics*, by Verba, Schlozman, and Brady (1995), and *"Mass Apathy" and Voluntary Social Participation in the United States*, by Bernard Barber (1980). Both try to understand civic involvement by examining the reasons for lack of participation in voluntary associations rather than finding reasons for such

29

participation. In some ways this has proven useful in understanding the obstacles to civic action in civil society; however, this approach does not examine the social histories and influences that lead to participation in civil society. It does not help explain why some citizens are engaged in the public lives of their communities, and it does not describe who they are or what influenced them to get involved.

To understand the influences and antecedents that lead to civic behavior and its development in young people, it is helpful to think of citizens as having civic careers. This provides a larger developmental framework that relates to Goffman's discussion of moral careers in *Asylums* (Goffman, 1961). He refers to careers in this usage as "any social strand of any person's course through life" (1961, p. 127). The notion of career allows an understanding of the movement between the personal and the public, the self and society (Goffman, 1961, p. 127). This broader perspective can refer to the development of skills, attitudes, and behaviors that meet the social expectations for participation in civil society and for the more generalized notions of citizenship in the United States. The idea of an individual having a "career" also suggests that all people begin life with certain genetic or innate possibilities that may or may not be fostered by their experiences and by the various socializing agents that lead to their formation as adults.

> A human organism born with potentialities of an enormously wide range is confronted by people who belong to particular class, ethnic, sex, linguistic, geographical and possibly religious groups, who subject him to a process of acculturation that inhibits some potentialities and encourages or allows others to develop. (Stacey, 1977, p. 2)

This process of career socialization, and the understanding of how these socializing agents function, is important in understanding how more conscious efforts might be made to promote active engagement in civil society. Again, while the literature written about political socialization does not directly discuss civil society, it does suggest significant influences that direct our thinking and actions within a sociopolitical context. By examining research on both socialization and involvement in voluntary associations, a framework for this book can be provided.

It is also necessary to examine related studies in other fields that focus on human development and civic engagement. The three studies mentioned earlier, by Paul Loeb (1999), Bill Berkowitz (1987), and Laurent Daloz, Cheryl Keen, James Keen, and Sharon Parks (1996), provide additional evidence for the significance of these socializing agents. These studies are also more similar in nature to the work here as they provide an understanding of how people come to understand their role in society and their responsibilities to enhance the lives of others and the well-being of their communities and the larger communities of which they are a part.

EXPLAINING INVOLVEMENT IN CIVIL SOCIETY

Explaining why people get involved in civil society and the various voluntary associations of civil society first requires an understanding of organizational involvement as a whole. Verba, Schlozman, and Brady (1995) were particularly interested in participation in political organizations, those that directly influenced governmental action (p. 9). However, they found that such involvement is related to other organizational relationships and experiences as well, so they looked at organizational involvement as a whole.

Through survey research, they found that organizational involvement is widespread in the United States (Verba, Schlozman, & Brady, 1995, p. 62). Seventy-nine percent of the respondents reported organizational involvement through membership or through financial contributions,[1] with 41 percent reporting four or more affiliations (p. 62). The survey findings also reported the following:

> Of those indicating some kind of affiliation with at least one organization, 65 percent reported that they have attended a meeting within the past twelve months; 42 percent reported that they are active members, that is, that they have served on a committee, given time for special projects, or helped organize meetings; 28 percent reported that, within the past five years, they have served on the board or been an officer of an organization with which they are still involved. (Verba, Schlozman, & Brady, 1995, p. 62)

Verba, Schlozman, and Brady (1995) also found that "the bulk of participation in charitable or social service organizations—nearly 80 percent—is limited to a [financial] contribution" (p. 64) as compared to other organizations in which attending meetings is an integral aspect of the association. The fact that 80 percent of the participation was limited to a financial contribution is important, since the subjects studied in this research represent the 20 percent who are more engaged in the activities of such civic-minded organizations. The individuals interviewed for this book provide time, effort, and energy to the success of the programs, projects, and organizations themselves. While they may not be recognized as leaders with official titles, these individuals are the people who get things done, often without any recognition beyond their reputation in the community.

The Logic of Noninvolvement

In both Verba, Schlozman, and Brady's (1995) and Barber's (1980) study, the logic of the research was to explore why individuals would not be involved in voluntary organizations of civil society. Barber's research focused on "mass apathy." He was trying to understand why Americans were not more engaged in political life. At the time he wrote his dissertation *"Mass Apathy" and Voluntary Social Participation in the United States,* he found the current explanations for mass apathy inadequate. He suggests that the research of the time "fails to take into account certain facts about institutional structure in general and certain fundamental features of the American social system in particular" (Barber, 1980, p. 3).

To explain mass apathy, Barber (1980) asked why individuals do not get involved in voluntary associations. He found that the lack of participation in voluntary associations and political life reflects a pattern of role conflict between job, family, and opportunities for involvement (p. 3). Many individuals fulfilling multiple roles simply did not have the time to take care of families, make a living, and volunteer their time. In fact, the first two roles, taking care of a family and making a living, took an obvious priority over involvement in voluntary associations. Another explanation, to be discussed in more detail later in this chapter, involved the organization of large, formal associations. Barber (1980) pointed out that the oligarchic nature of such organizations serves to dissuade individuals from being actively involved.

In his concluding chapter, Barber (1980) suggested three conceptual categories for the analysis of voluntary participation in civil society: values, institutional or social structure, and motivation (p. 254). While he understood these categories as being interrelated, "for certain analytic purposes" (p. 255) they can be seen as independent. For example, social structure, particularly class, influences value systems and motivational levels, but not in all cases. Barber provided the following example regarding social activism:

> Although activism is commonly thought to involve all three elements—ideological conviction, behavioral hyperactivity, and enthusiastic sentiments—it need not. Among the sect of Jehovah's Witnesses, for example, strong convictions and persistent behavioral activity occur without the revivalistic sentiments that attach to some religious activism. (Barber, 1980, p. 255)

In the category of social structure, class has been found to be a major determinant of participation in voluntary associations, by both rate or the number of organizations one is involved with and the type or specific purposes that the organization serves (i.e., professional, recreational, etc.) (Komarovsky, 1946, as cited in Barber, 1980, p. 70). A higher income also increases the likelihood of involvement in local organizations (Lundberg et al., 1934, as cited in Barber,

1980, p. 71). Interestingly, class is also related to gender in explaining membership in voluntary associations, according to Warner (1941, as cited in Barber, 1980). Warner found that "women had proportionally more membership than the men in his three upper classes, and the situation was reversed for the three lower classes" (Barber, 1980, p. 65). Class is also related to the educational level achieved, and Barber cites two studies that related education to membership in voluntary associations (Komarovsky, 1946, and Goldhamer, 1943, as cited in Barber, 1980, p. 77).

Another factor regarding voluntary participation in civil society had to do with historical events. World War II influenced Barber's research. He found that people's civic involvement changed during periods of crisis, and that for some this change was permanent.

> Thus, certain generalizations are apparent. There was a very great increase in the number of volunteers in social work during the war owing to changes in community attitudes about social participation and to changes in role obligations that ordinarily prevent such participation. When the war crisis was ended and when former obligations prevailed again, there was a return to the old pattern of participation, probably with some net gain in the direction of more participation, however. There was also during the war a change in the character of the volunteer population. What had formerly consisted entirely of middle-class women had become, more nearly, a cross-section of the society. (Barber, 1980, p. 191)

In his research and in his review of the literature, Barber (1980) did not focus on motivation. His main arguments focused on the reasons people did not get involved rather than why they did. Therefore, motivation for involvement did not enter into his research.

Verba, Schlozman, and Brady (1995) also used the logic of explaining noninvolvement rather than understanding why individuals participate politically.

> In thinking about why some people are active while others are not, we find it helpful to invert the usual question and to ask instead why people do *not* [italics in original] take part in politics. Three answers immediately suggest themselves: because they can't; because they don't want to; or because nobody asked. (Verba, Schlozman, & Brady, 1995, p. 15)

Verba, Schlozman, and Brady (1995) explain that people cannot get involved in voluntary associations associated with governmental action because they lack the time, money, or skills. These individuals do not want to participate in such associations because of a lack of interest, concern, knowledge, or a sense of efficacy. Lastly, they are isolated from the networks of recruitment, therefore nobody asked them to get involved in these associations (p. 16).

Verba, Schlozman, and Brady's (1995) findings regarding voluntary participation in civil society reflected much of the earlier political socialization research. Like Barber (1980), they found that the priorities of family and work often precluded activity in voluntary associations. However, Verba, Schlozman, and Brady (1995) suggested that the family, along with school, is critical in laying the foundations for civic skill development and psychological engagement in politics. After these foundations have been laid, "the institutional affiliations of adults—on the job, in non-political organizations, and in religious institutions—provide additional opportunities for the acquisition of politically relevant resources and the enhancement of a sense of psychological engagement with politics" (Verba, Schlozman, & Brady, 1995, pp. 3–4). Throughout this process, factors such as class, gender, and race determine which organizations influence the individual and can predict future involvement and organizational contacts.

Motivations

Unlike Barber, Verba, Schlozman, and Brady (1995) do spend some time exploring the possible motivations for voluntary action in civil society. They suggest four different motivations for involvement in voluntary associations. The first motivations are "*selective material benefits* such as jobs, career advancement, or help with a personal or family problem" (Verba, Schlozman, & Brady, 1995, p. 109, emphasis in original). These benefits are not related to the activity itself. Verba, Schlozman, and Brady (1995) offer the following as examples of selective material benefits:

> "The chance to further by job or career."
> "I might want to get help from an official (from the organization, etc.) on a personal or family problem."
> "I might want to run for office someday."
> "I might want to get a job with the government someday."
> "The direct services provided to (church or organization) members."
> "The recreational activities offered by the organization." (p. 111)

The second motivation for involvement in voluntary associations is selective social gratifications. These social gratifications refer to "the enjoyment of working with others or the excitement of politics" (Verba, Schlozman, & Brady, 1995, p. 109) and cannot be separated from the activity of the association itself. Some items mentioned include:

> "I find it exciting."
> "The chance to be with people I enjoy."
> "The chance to meet important and influential people."

"The chance for recognition from people I respect."
"I did not want to say no to someone who asked." (p. 111)

The third motivation for involvement in voluntary associations is selective civic gratifications, which are intrinsic rewards that satisfy a sense of responsibility or a desire to contribute to the welfare of a specific community. Civic gratification is derived from the acts themselves (Verba, Schlozman, & Brady, 1995, p. 109). Verba, Schlozman, and Brady (1995) do point out that reports of this form of motivation may be due to subjects' desire to project a positive self-image. Some of the items that are mentioned include:

"My duty as a citizen."
"I am the kind of person who does my share."
"The chance to make the community or nation a better place to live."
(p. 112)

The last identified motivation for involvement in voluntary associations refers to collective outcomes or results that relate directly to influencing governmental policy through public policy or through the election of a particular candidate. Unlike the other motivations, collective outcomes can suffer from the free-rider problem or the idea that some benefit from others' activities with no cost to themselves (p. 110).

Of all these motivations for involvement in voluntary associations, Verba, Schlozman, and Brady (1995) found that the proportion of activists who mentioned social gratifications to explain their behavior is much higher than expected, based on the literature discussing collective action (p. 117). This literature tends to emphasize selected material benefits as the primary motivator in voluntary social action. Verba, Schlozman, and Brady (1995) refer to David Knoke's research, which suggests that "members who were attracted to an organization for normative or social inducements were more likely to be active participants in the organization, while those who were attracted to more selective benefits were less likely to be active in the organization" (see note 40, p. 127).

Activists, those who contribute time to organizations, voting or campaigning, or community issues or concerns, more frequently reported that civic gratifications were more important than material benefits or social gratifications (Verba, Schlozman, & Brady, 1995, p. 117). Often subjects refer to "doing one's share and making the community or nation a better place to live" (p. 132). However, the type of involvement is significant for those subjects who mention civic gratification alone. Of those subjects engaged in voting, 71 percent mentioned civic gratification as their only motivation. For subjects who were active in nonpolitical organizations, 14 percent mentioned civic gratification as their only motivator, and the same motivation was noted for 18 percent of those active in church organizations (Verba, Schlozman, & Brady, 1995, p. 118). The findings in David Knoke's (1988, as cited in Verba, Schlozman, and Brady, 1995) study and in Verba, Schlozman, and Brady's (1995) research suggest that the motivations for activity in nonpolitical organizations and churches, while partly related to civic gratifications, also rely heavily on social gratification.

Bellah, Madsen, Sullivan, Swidler, & Tipton (1985) suggest that most people get involved in social institutions to achieve their self-interest, or because they feel "an affinity with certain others" (p. 167). In terms of motivations, this notion of an affinity for others could be considered the same as Verba, Schlozman, and Brady's (1995) concept of social gratification, while the notion of getting involved through self-interest could be considered similar to Verba, Schlozman, and Brady's (1995) concept of selective material benefits. However, Bellah et al.'s understanding of self-interest is more reflective of Tussman's (1997) concept of enlightened self-interest.

> "Getting involved" for most of those we have met so far . . . has two fundamental meanings. It expresses a genuine concern for one's local community, a concern expressed in working for its betterment and caring for those in need within it. . . .
>
> The second meaning of getting involved has to do with the protection of one's interests, so vivid in the consciousness of the concerned citizen, but never far from the consciousness of the town father either. (Bellah et al., 1985, p. 191)

This idea of the "town father" or "town mother" incorporates a sense of understanding how one's interests are contingent upon the community as a whole. The town father was concerned with the investment that he or she had made in the community, be it a business or a family. To realize that one's personal investments are tied to a community—what Tussman (1997) calls "enlightened self-interest"—requires an individual to not only see how his or her personal interest relates directly to the community and its members but to have information on this community and how its needs fit into larger political contexts such as the state or the nation. Within these social contexts, to have such information requires that there be civil practices that allow for shared discussion or debate on the definition of the common good.

In *The Call of Service*, by Robert Coles (1993), the motivation to perform service is described within a moral context. Coles was influenced by his parents as well as by other more prominent role models like Dorothy Day. Among other things, he wanted to explore "the many rationales, impulses, and values served in the implementation of a particular effort" (Coles, 1993, p. xxiv). By service, Coles was referring to the volunteer efforts of individuals to serve those in need or to make the world a better place. While Coles's study is important to this research, there are differences between the kinds of volunteerism being performed. Typically, Coles was referring to individuals who serve members outside of their community, and often outside of their class. In this book, the subjects studied are members of the community in which they serve. Of course, they too may be serving individuals who are not of the same socioeconomic status, but these are still people with whom the subjects have some contact in their daily lives. Exceptions will include those subjects whose church work often carries them beyond the immediate community. In the context of church and religion, volunteerism often takes on a more moral dimension, as Coles discussed.

Coles (1993) suggested that "the very definition or notion of service has to do with the ethical and spiritual assumptions that inform a family's life" (Coles, 1993, p. 7). He looked at his subjects to try to understand the moral energy he had seen in his parents and in his own role models. In keeping with other research on voluntary social action, Coles (1993) also found multiple reasons to explain why people choose to perform service for others. However, he felt that service began with the values and ideals that inform action.

> He [Coles is referring to one of his subjects] had carried to the South the values he had learned in a white, fairly well-to-do, secular home up North. Or, it might be said, those values had carried him to Dixie, and though he might not have dwelt on them explicitly, they were a part of his life, as he acknowledged, and they help us understand what he was doing, what others like him were doing and continue to do. (Coles, 1993, p. 34)

However, Coles found that those doing the service often began to focus more on the relations and personal contacts they had with those in need of assistance; while they say it is a matter of belief, it becomes a matter of genuine concern for others (p. 38).

Coles (1993) also mentioned the influence of events or circumstances for explaining service. He described a situation in which two mothers worked together to offer support to their daughters who shared a very serious illness. In the process, they began to help each other in different ways; they began to explore each other's worlds. In another case, a man's friend invited him to join him in working at a nursing home. The friend's priest suggested that this work might help the friend deal with his father's death. After they both do this, the experience becomes part of their lives. "Whatever the prompting circumstances, one human being responds to another in private gestures that morally inform certain lives" (Coles, 1993, p. 53).

Similar to Coles (1993), Daloz et al. (1996) and Loeb (1999) tend to focus on the moral or intellectual dimensions of human development in explaining motivations for involvement. Loeb suggests that those he interviewed "keep going because participation is essential to their dignity, to their very identity, to the person they see in the mirror" (Loeb, 1999, p. 339). In *Common Fire: Leading Lives of Commitment in a Complex World* (1996), Daloz et al. begin by finding people who meet an intellectual criterion that allows them to "understand the larger, systemic implications of their work and had a critical perspective on their own culture" (p. 5). Their subjects also had already established long-term commitments working toward some common good and were more likely to have an identity more absorbed by their civic career than any other career.

Of course, being asked or being recruited into such organizations or work is a major factor in understanding participation in civic society. Verba, Schlozman, and Brady (1995) discovered that many subjects began their involvement in voluntary associations by being asked to join or participate (p. 133). These subjects were recruited through their personal connections that were part of a larger social network structured around class and ethnicity (pp. 140–149). In this understanding of recruitment and networking, it becomes clear that early socialization and access to resources are key to future opportunities. To begin to understand this early socialization and the developmental processes related to participation in voluntary associations of civil society, it is important to look at the research available on political socialization.

POLITICAL SOCIALIZATION

Defining political socialization first requires an understanding of the socialization process itself. "*Socialization* refers to the developmental processes whereby each person acquires the knowledge, skills, beliefs, values, attitudes, and dispositions which enable him or her to function as a more or less effective, though not inevitably compliant, member of society" (Stacey, 1977, p. 2, emphasis in original). Compliance is important to a definition of political socialization. Roberta Sigel states that political socialization "refers to the process by which people learn to adopt the norms, values, attitudes, and behaviors accepted and practiced by the ongoing system" (Sigel, 1970, p. xii). This does not allow for individual agency to reject or refuse total indoctrination into the social and political order. Greenstein talks about this distinction in his definition of political socialization.

> Narrowly conceived, political socialization is the deliberate inculcation of political information, values, and practices by instructional agents who have been formally charged with this responsibility. A broader conception would encompass all political learning, formal and informal, deliberate and unplanned, at every stage of the life cycle, including not only explicitly political learning but also nominal non-political learning that affects political behavior, such as

the learning of politically relevant social attitudes and the acquisition of politically relevant personality characteristics. (Greenstein, 1968, as cited in Stacey, 1977, p. 3)

In this book, the broader definition of socialization will be used. The assumption being made is that socialization or, more specifically, political socialization, is not always a conscious or an intentional transference. The social institutions and the people who run them are not always aware of how they influence others. The very structure of authority and the responsibility of families, schools, churches, and employment may determine which values, attitudes, and beliefs young people adopt. The fact that parents, teachers, ministers, and employers do not always consciously socialize others does not mean that they do not consciously promote certain values and attitudes; it means that they do not always promote values and attitudes for the purposes of political behavior. They are less conscious about the broader political contexts and more conscious about the particular social contexts in which they know those who may be influenced. The transference of values, attitudes, and beliefs must also be understood with an appreciation for individual differences and the unique development that social meaning has for each individual.

In thinking about the many social contexts in which we interact with others, the concept of primary and secondary groups is helpful. Most people, and especially young people, have their early experiences of the world structured by primary groups (Thompson & Hickey, 1994, p. 97). These groups are those in which an individual has frequent, face-to-face interactions and with whom there is some commitment to relationships (p. 151). Two particularly important primary groups are the family and peer groups; these groups help the individual form the basis for an understanding of the self within a social context (Cooley, 1909, 22, as cited in Thompson & Hickey, 1994, p. 151). Secondary groups serve some instrumental purpose for members. These groups are formed so all members will receive some benefit or avoid some costs. They are more formal and impersonal (Thompson & Hickey, 1994, p. 151) and more relevant to the experience of adult socialization. Such groups can include religious, professional or work-related, and political associations. Both primary and secondary groups help form the basis for social behavior.

Based on Mead (1964, as cited in Hearn, 1997), Frank Hearn (1997) elaborated on how secondary groups help promote moral cooperative relationships between people and their primary groups.

Of particular importance are local associations established to further the needs of families, communities, and their members. Amidst the close personal relations supported by these social settings, the individual defines herself in part with reference to those significant and generalized others with whom she interacts so that her self-interest is generally compatible with the interests of others. In these contexts, Mead (1964: 249–82) argued, people are able to cultivate their sympathetic and charitable impulses, to perfect their cooperative skills, and to develop their capacity to arrive at a set of common purposes and ideals which set the terms by which they regulate their lives. (Hearn, 1997, pp. 160–161)

Hearn argues that what Mead and Durkheim had in mind was not the oppressive associations of premodern societies but associations based on a "morality of cooperation" that is more reflective of the liberal practices of modern society (Hearn, 1997, pp. 160–164). The concept of morality of cooperation is from the work of Jean Piaget (1965, as cited in Hearn, 1997), who identified two key stages in the moral development of children.

[The first] is characterized by submission to authority and externality of rules. It is a stage of "strict law," in which the bare fact of infraction, regardless of context or intent, warrants corrective punishment. In the second stage . . . there is greater awareness of reciprocity, equal treatment, and mutual respect among peers, as well as an increased capacity to distinguish a just rule from one that is merely authoritative. (Selznick, 1992, 165, as cited in Hearn, 1997, p. 161)

Such a morality negates "tension between society—comprising primordial and organic ties and the local, communal, mutual, voluntaristic groups that develop around them—and the equality, justice, and individualism promised by a modernity driven by purposively constructed market and state organizations" (Hearn, 1997, p. 162).

As we examine the civic careers of the subjects in this book in chapters 5 and 6, the significance of these various socializing groups or agencies and their capacity to provide a moral direction for behavior will be discussed, particularly with reference to the development of the values and virtues that lead to civic behavior. The groups that have been traditionally examined as agents of socialization include family, church, peers, education, media, work, and participation in voluntary associations.

Family

The influence of the family on children is significant in that it is the first social context for childhood socialization. In particular, the child's moral development is shaped by the acceptance or rejection the child receives from his or her parents according to Sears, Maccoby, and Levin (1957, as cited in Davies, 1977,

p. 165). The internalization of control, somewhat akin to Piaget's morality of collaboration, is more likely to occur when the child receives positive and negative attention from the parent versus material rewards and physical punishment (Sears et al., 1957, as cited in Davies, 1977, pp. 165–166). Early experiences in the family may also lead to how the child views the world and herself or himself; her or his experience may tell her or him that the world is hostile or friendly and may influence her or his perceptions of having power or being powerless (Davies, 1977, pp. 162–168). Families can actually set the stage for the valuing of future social opportunities or contexts.

> Social participation is, to a considerable degree, a family trait. Family members participate in social activities if other family members are participators; they do not if other family members are non-participators. (Anderson, W.A., 1946, p. 253, as cited in Barber, 1980, p. 61)

Family life is also seen as a major factor by Queener in his 1949 study on attitude formation (as cited in Hyman, 1959). However, Queener provides a theory for his results. He believes that individuals imitate some model or person who provides the cues for attitude formation. The model is only followed if he or she has prestige, which comes from the control of rewards and punishments of behavior. Given this theory, it is clear why the family provides the first social context in which the child will select his or her first role model. Queener also makes the point that if individual models are of equal prestige then the more proximate source is followed. Again, this gives the advantage to family members at first. Later on in the child's development, peers become more significant. As the child's needs for social recognition and identity grow, she or he looks to those who have achieved such awards. Such role models would be more likely to be her or his peers. In a sense, most individuals develop a variety of social contexts in which new behaviors are developed and more likely influenced by others (Hyman, 1959, pp. 98–103).

Parental models may also have very different motivations. Parental motivations to socialize their children into dominant social pathways often reflect family history (Weissberg & Joslyn, 1977, pp. 47–48). For example, immigrants wanted their children to adapt to what they perceived as American culture and language, whereas families who were nonvoluntarily brought into this country, such as African Americans, might be less interested in socializing children into European-American traditions. This has a multitude of implications for other socializing agents as well, particularly education.[2]

Many of the studies mentioned in Renshon (1977) that examine the influence of parents and family life are dated and do not address the changes in the structure of the contemporary American family.[3] Bloche (1953, as cited in Hyman, 1959, p. 128) remarks that in French peasant society, both parents must work, so the grandparents raise the children. He says that this is the reason for the traditionalism in many peasant societies. In modern American society, the necessity of two-income families and single-parent families also suggests that parents may not be raising children properly. Children are either raising themselves, grandparents or pseudo grandparents/parents are doing the job, or contracted day care centers are fulfilling this critical societal function. What this means to socialization and the early preparation of children for citizenship is an area for speculation. The shift in basic child care could signify a return to traditional values of grandparents or children who are ambiguous about their values and themselves. In any case, if it continues, it signals a declining influence for many parents.

American parents are also not particularly interested in the conscious socialization of political values (Beck, 1977, p. 139). They do influence general ideals about culture and society (Keniston, 1968, as cited in Orum, 1989, p. 280), and if they are particularly interested in politics, they probably have more of an influence on their children's beliefs (Jennings & Niemi, 1974, as cited in Orum, 1989, p. 280). For example, if parents provide some form of political stimulation such as discussion or debate, they may help encourage political interest (Verba, Schlozman, & Brady, 1995, p. 436). In Daloz et al. (1996), the authors suggest that family dialogue was significant to their subjects in that three-quarters had family dinners together that often included "lively conversations" (p. 110). They further suggest that through "dialogue and constructive engagement with others, young people grow more able to sense, and to construct at least roughly, how the world may actually look and feel through the eyes of another" (p.111), something that is critical in their model of citizenship and very much related to enlightened self-interest.

Much of the socialization that parents do is more generalized in regard to larger social contexts and only later develops into having political significance. In other words, while parents may not intentionally teach values and behavior that are "political," values they teach and behaviors they promote have increasing political implications as children begin to have more contact with secondary groups. For example, in Daloz et al. (1996), commitment to the common good is said to arise in families with a "healthy sense of trust and agency, which in turn grows from the experience of being loved and the opportunity to care" (p. 26). They also suggest that in the "mini-commons of the home, we learn in a preverbal, bone-deep way, fundamental dispositions toward generosity or meanness, respect or scorn, equality or domination" (p. 27), all of which influence our conception of ourselves and of others within public life.

Parents may also act as civic role models. Loeb (1999) suggests that if "we're involved in our community, speak openly about the causes and principles we believe in, and invite our children along when appropriate, they'll get the message on their own, even if they can't articulate it until they're older" (p. 179). Daloz et al. (1996) also suggest that parental behavior may not be the sole determinant of later civic involvement, but it certainly increases the likelihood (p. 17).

Church

Church life may also be significant to early social experiences of young people, particularly because it is so value specific. Daloz et al. (1996) found that the majority of people who fit their model of public commitment had been greatly influenced by the church. One of their subjects spoke about the significance of church groups where there was an "affirmation of honesty and integrity and pushing you beyond the bounds of what you used to think" (p. 42). They also found that for those "who describe themselves as having been positively influenced by religious institutions, their experience seems to have given them a secure sense of belonging to a particular people who were also a part of a yet wider world" (p. 34). There continues to be more and more research on the significance of church life to socialization, and the realization that people with strong religious convictions are "more involved in social causes and community activities" (Berkowitz, 1987, p. 317).

Verba, Schlozman, and Brady (1995) discuss the significance of church life particularly from a sense of skill development and organizational opportunity. However, the emphasis of their research is on how these experiences lead to voting patterns and involvement in shaping public policy, whereas Daloz et al. (1996) find that these leadership opportunities within the church supported the development of many of their subjects who played key roles in voluntary associations within civil society (p. 42).

Bellah et al. (1985) conducted a qualitative study on American communities and individual beliefs and practices related to public life. As part of their study, they found that church life was significant to their subjects.

> For all of them, religion provides a conception, even if rudimentary, of how one should live. They all share the idea that one's obligations to God involve one's life at work as well as in the family, what one does as a citizen as well as how one treats one's friends. (Bellah et al., 1985, p. 239)

Unfortunately, religion and existence outside of the church can create problems for public life, since there is a tension between individual spirituality and religion's significance to "the whole of life" (Bellah et al., 1985, p. 248). Bellah quotes Parker J. Palmer:

> Perhaps the most important ministry the church can have in the renewal of public life is a "ministry of paradox": not to resist the inward turn of American spirituality on behalf of effective public action, *but to deepen and direct and discipline that inwardness in the light of faith* until God leads us back to a vision of the public and to faithful action on the public's behalf. (Palmer, 1981, as cited in Bellah et al., 1985, p. 248, emphasis in original)

In other words, the internalization of faith can and must be strengthened through action in public life. This perspective on faith is reflective of the motivations mentioned by Coles (1993).

Peers

The influence of peers changes through human development. During early childhood, peers play a role in the development of patterns of cooperation and moral judgment (Kohlberg, 1969, Piaget, 1950, and Riccards, 1973, as cited in Silbiger, 1977, p. 182) and, as mentioned by Queener (1949, as cited in Hyman, 1959, pp. 161–163), peers become more significant as children look for social recognition and identity outside of the family. This is particularly true with lower-class families. In such families, children do not always see their parents as reliable role models; they tend to put more emphasis on peer models from middle- to upper-class families (Silbiger, 1977, p. 175). Peers also become more significant in the discussion of media events as children get older (Meine, 1941, as cited in Hyman, 1959).

In time, as individual identity begins to stabilize, peers have less influence and individuals tend to identify with those peers who are most like themselves (Brim, 1966, as cited in Silbiger, 1977, p. 174). Silbiger (1977, p. 172) also points out that peer influence occurs at a time in which there are many other influencing agents of socialization, therefore, peers often are reinforcers of socialization.

The greatest peer influence takes place when new contexts or "objects" occur in different life stages (Silbiger, 1977). For example, when young people are faced with new problems or situations, without previous social learning, they will look to peers for direction. This occurs when students are learning new group roles as well, such as leadership and team play (Silbiger, 1977, p. 184). Typically, peers who have the greatest influence are those peers who are perceived by those who choose them as role models as being attractive and as having a potential for a prolonged relationship (Silbiger, 1977, p. 177). Such peers are also more influential if they have prestige, according to Queener's model (Queener, 1949, as cited in Hyman, 1959).

Education

Education is perhaps the most significant form of formal, public influence, and its sway has grown due to an increase in the years of education that people attain (Hyman, 1959, p. 133). As early as 1914, teachers were shown to have an increasing influence on their students with regard to political values at the same time parental influence was declining (Hall, 1914, as cited in Hyman, 1959, p. 99). However, educational curricula are often a reflection of community values, since local communities and state governments usually control what is taught. This suggests that school influence provides a "redundancy in cues, rather than competition with other agents" (Beck, 1977, p. 131).

In terms of political orientation, education is seen as significant in exposing students to a greater variety of viewpoints.

> The hypothesis is advanced that education, by exposing the individual to a *variety of viewpoints* and a diversity of information, creates the basis for rational decisions about politics and thus attenuates the influence of such nonrational factors as family tradition. No strong evidence in support of this hypothesis is presented, although some suggestive findings are consistent with it. (Hyman, 1959, p. 145, emphasis in original)

While examining research regarding education and political socialization, many studies are contradictory or have significant flaws. Beck (1977, p. 131) points out that the research done on early education "where the influence of school might be expected to be greatest" has generally resulted in findings for the null hypothesis. Beck outlines four categories of research in schools (1977, p. 128): formal instruction and routines, contributions of teachers as individuals, extracurricular activities, and peer group environment.

Patrick (1977, pp. 193–196) also provides four "dimensions" for political education and socialization in schools: knowledge as it relates to information, concepts, and judgments about government and politics; intellectual skills, such as the ability to describe, explain, and evaluate political phenomena or to make moral judgments and evaluate the moral judgments of others; political participation skills, or the ability to work with others toward a goal to negotiate, compromise, bargain, make decisions, and influence others; and political attitudes, or "an internal state which affects an individual's choice of action toward some objective, person, or event" (Gagne & Briggs, 1974, as cited in Patrick, 1977, p. 195).

In a more recent work, Verba, Schlozman, and Brady (1995) point out the indirect influence of education on political participation. For example, higher levels of education lead to better or higher paying jobs that provide more resources such as time, money, and interpersonal connections. These resources yield more opportunities to participate in society and politics. Student engagement in school activities can also provide the skills and a "propensity for activity" later in life (p. 432) and can enhance confidence in students' ability to exert influence in social change (Almond & Verba, 1963). In fact, it is the experience of school, what Patrick calls the "hidden curriculum" (1977, p. 204), that can often shape students' understandings of their roles and abilities to influence public life. Unfortunately, the tension between providing students with the cognitive and participatory skills necessary for democracy and the needs of school administrators to maintain control over the lives of the student body and the formal process of sequential grade structures stand in contradiction to one another (McNeil, 1988).

Ironically, the fact that higher education leads to better jobs may also inhibit the possibilities for becoming engaged in community life (Verba, Schlozman, & Brady, 1995). Often these jobs require employees to be mobile in order to advance. These families fail to become integrated into the community and are less likely to be engaged in local organizations (Verba, Schlozman, and Brady, 1995, p. 455).

Media

Like education, the influence of media is filtered by a variety of other agents of socialization, such as family and peers, shaping both the use and interpretation of media. According to Beck (1977), "the brunt of the research evidence is that the impact of the media seems to be confined to increasing the level of information about the political world" (p. 135). Chaffee, Jackson-Beeck, Durall, and Wilson (1977) suggest that there are four conclusions to be drawn from the research regarding young people and the media:

1. Media is the principal source of political information for young people.
2. The dominant source of mass media for political learning is newspapers and television, and age and socioeconomic status vary this influence.
3. Young people attribute mass media to have considerable influence on their political opinions.
4. Children do not adopt the political media norms of their parents, and the habits they do develop persist into adulthood. (pp. 227–229)

It is also important to examine the effect of different forms of media on socialization. Bellah et al. (1992, p. 148) found that children spend more time with radio and television than they do in school. With the expansion of the Internet, the question of how much time children spend with "virtual friends" versus immediate friends also arises. For Bellah et al. (1992, p. 149), the increasing access to media makes the interpretation of events even more difficult as the audience becomes overwhelmed with information. They also suggest that the media shapes our identities, as we see ourselves as part of a global world in which we have little or no real understanding or meaning. The whole notion of identity is further complicated as young people create "virtual identities" in various Internet chat rooms.

The ability of the media to shape individual identity is important. Boyte (1989) argues that commercial media, along with governmental agencies, frame the viewer or listener as a consumer or client, and that this understanding has significant effects on civic behavior. Instead of seeing oneself as part of a community for which one has both rights and responsibilities, someone who sees herself or himself as a client and a consumer sees community life as being controlled from without and not from within her or his control. She or he sees all mediating institutions as places of economic exchange, not as places in which she or he has a stake and a responsibility to determine.

Work

In adulthood and in life beyond the family, the workplace becomes the most significant agent of socialization. Sigel and Hoskin (1977, p. 272) provide three perspectives for exploring the influence of the workplace:

1. The socializing effect of the workplace itself;
2. The extent to which certain occupations give rise to or are associated with specific political beliefs; and
3. The socializing effect of occupational status.

Unfortunately, most of the research in political socialization focuses on children and young adults and fails to address the workplace. The dominant paradigm for most of this research was that children, once socialized, develop cognitive frameworks that remain with them the rest of their lives. While some frameworks may persist, as adults take on new roles or are engaged in new social contexts they may begin a socialization process anew. As adults face new social contexts, they may rely on old frameworks to determine their behaviors or adopt new frameworks, depending on the perceived functionality of these other frameworks and the motivation of the individual (Sigel, 1989).

In terms of maintaining early patterns of socialization, Sigel and Hoskin (1977, p. 282) point out that even occupational choices may be a reflection of earlier patterns of socialization. Individuals pursue work opportunities that reflect their values and attitudes. This may explain why workers in the same occupation tend to share the same political orientations (Sigel & Hoskin, 1977, p. 274). However, there is little systematic research available to explore this problem, according to Sigel and Hoskin (1977).

Some significant research has been undertaken to look at the relationship between occupation and status vis-à-vis political behavior. Some observations are that:

> (1) the higher the prestige of a given occupation, the higher the social status enjoyed by its practitioners; (2) the higher the status of individuals, the more politically active they are likely to be (Verba & Nie, 1974); (3) the more active people are politically, the greater the variety of access points to political power brokers, and the more frequently these are used (Verba & Nie, 1974); (4) the higher the status, the greater the likelihood that the occupants' political views will tend toward the conservative—with the possible exception of views on civil liberties and civil rights (Stouffer, 1955). (Sigel & Hoskin, 1977, p. 282)

Lipset (1960, as cited in Sigel & Hoskin, 1977, p. 282) finds the opposite political patterns among low-prestige occupations. People with low social status are less active in politics. They have little input into politics and less access to political leaders. They also tend to be more liberal on economic issues and more conservative on cultural issues.

Participation in Voluntary Associations

People who currently participate in community associations often belong to more than one group. In fact, they usually have a history of community and organizational involvement. Typically this involvement tends to intensify in overall demands or personal commitment. Given this pattern, it is important to examine how socialization affects such participation in voluntary organizations. However, when we examine the literature about the relationship of participation in voluntary organizations and socialization, the meaning of voluntary organizations is somewhat different from the organizations examined in this research. This book attempts to study involvement in civil society within a communal context; involvement in voluntary associations is connected to the immediate community.

Some of the more significant research on participation in voluntary associations was done by Bernard Barber (1980), who tried to understand the "mass apathy" of American citizens in the early and mid-1940s. He examined three areas of citizen participation, which included activity in "voluntary associations, non-voting behavior, and voluntary participation in community welfare activities" (p. 3). Barber made a clear distinction between voluntary associations and the communities in which citizens live:

> Associations are organizations for the pursuit of these limited, specific ends. An association consists of a group of people joined together for the achieve-

ment of an explicit purpose which they have in common. They are brought together simply ad hoc , for this purpose, and may have no other interests in common besides that for which the association has been formed. In a community, typically, there is a multiplicity and interpenetration of ends and no explicit statement of their existence and segregation. (Barber, 1980, p. 30)

Barber (1980) was referring to a very particular kind of voluntary activity that is more reflective of the idea of social work.

There is, in the United States, a long and very important tradition of voluntary participation in community welfare activities. Indeed, the care of the needy in all its forms, inclusively denoted here as "social work," originated largely in the purposes and efforts of private persons who volunteered to aid their less fortunate fellow-citizens. (Barber, 1980, p. 178)

Unlike the idea of voluntary associations presented by Barber, this book focuses on those associations that begin within the mediating institutions that are integral to community life (i.e., schools, churches, neighborhood associations, volunteer fire departments, etc.). Also, unlike Barber's (1980) understanding of voluntary participation in community welfare activities, this research is interested in the individuals and organizations that have an impact on the communities in which they place themselves, or in which they have a sense of belonging. This includes organizations that enhance community life or public life for all members, not necessarily just the "needy." Fundamentally, this book focuses on understanding participation in social organizations that are rooted in the community and that promote the welfare of that community as a primary mission, with expanded interest in surrounding communities as those interests and missions become interrelated.

Another distinction between political and nonpolitical activity must also be made. Verba, Schlozman, and Brady (1995) look at voluntary activity in the United States with a focus on political activity or participation, which they define as "activity that is intended to or has the consequence of affecting, either directly or indirectly, government action" (p. 9). They "consider" a range of activities, including "work in election campaigns, contributions to campaigns and other political causes, informal contacts activity in local communities, contacts with public officials, affiliation with political organizations, attendance at demonstrations or protests, and service on local governing bodies as school or zoning boards" (p. 9). However, Verba, Schlozman, and Brady (1995) find that the "boundary between political and non-political activity is by no means clear, an aspect of political and social life in America that complicates the analysis of political and non-political participation" (p. 40).

This book examines participation within a specific community. While the participation of subjects in this study may reflect "political" participation (i.e., school boards and local town boards), it also reflects nonpolitical participation (i.e., church groups and Rotary clubs). Some organizations are both voluntary and community based but are also heavily regulated by the state, including volunteer ambulance and fire departments. What these organizations have in common is a commitment to a specific community, a community in which these people live and raise their families.

Many of the people studied in this book would be insulted if their activity was labeled "political." This reflected Bellah et al.'s (1985) findings that many people find politics "morally unsavory" (p. 199).

> For a good number of those we talked to, *politics* connotes something morally unsavory, as though voluntary involvement were commendable and fulfilling up to the point at which it enters the realm of office holding, campaigning, and organized negotiating. Their judgments of public involvement and responsibility turn negative when they extend beyond the bounds of their local concerns. (Bellah et al., 1985, p. 199, emphasis in original)

While the focus of this book is on active participation in local, civic-minded organizations, it is important to reflect on the findings of the other studies discussed in this chapter as they relate to the question of the socialization of involvement in all voluntary associations. As mentioned in chapter 2, civil society theorists believe that community involvement leads to civic virtue and enlightened self-interest. This is reflected in the work of Bellah et al. (1985), who found that "getting involved can lead to a deepened conception of society and the role of citizenship within it" (p. 192). In and of itself, given the right social contexts, this would suggest that involvement leads to conceptual changes about the role of citizenship and to an increase in the opportunity for future engagement in civil society.

Barber (1980) also found that members in many associations are not regularly involved in large associations and become less engaged in public life due to their experiences. While discussing trade unions, he found that there is

> a "push" away from active participation because of the nature of the organization of the voluntary association. Because of the division of functions among members, in short, because of the existence of the kind of formal organization . . . a minority can achieve the interests of the association with the majority participating only minimally. (Barber, 1980, pp. 81–82)

Although Barber does not explore this anti-democratic organizational tendency in much detail, one aspect of socialization might be the negative impact of involvement in large-scale organizations. Certainly if individuals seek meaningful action within the organization only to find it controlled by an elite, then the possibility of future involvement might be reduced.

Although Verba, Scholzman, and Brady (1995) were not directly concerned with nonpolitical voluntary associations, they realized that "the bulk of voluntary participation in this country takes place outside of politics" (p. 79), and that this participation does provide members with the civic skills necessary for future engagement in political associations.

> The development of civic skills does not cease with the end of schooling but can continue throughout adulthood. These non-political institutions offer many opportunities to acquire, or improve, organizational or communications skills in the context of activities that have nothing to do with politics. Managing the firm's move to new quarters, coordinating the volunteers for the Heart Fund drive, or arranging the details for a tour by the church children's choir—all these undertakings represent opportunities in non-political settings to learn, maintain, or refine civic skills. In short, those who develop skills in an environment removed from politics are likely to become politically competent. (Verba, Schlozman, & Brady, 1995, p. 310)

In fact, their findings suggest that participation in nonpolitical associations, particularly the church, is "much less structured by income, race, or ethnicity than is political activity" (Verba, Schlozman, & Brady, 1995, p. 317). Participation with churches can actually "compensate" for the lack of opportunity for job-related civic training available for those in low-level jobs.

Socialization as a Process

The significance of each of these agents of socialization varies widely. Clearly, civic participation in civil society comes from many different types of experiences. The influence of these agents and experiences begins early in the development of the individual.

> The foundations for future political involvements are laid early in life—in the family and in school. Later on, the institutional affiliations of adults—on the job, in non-political organizations, and in religious institutions—provide additional opportunities for the acquisition of politically relevant resources and the enhancement of a sense of psychological engagement with politics. (Verba, Schlozman, & Brady, 1995, pp. 3–4)

If we examine these agents of socialization, we see that the family is a very significant social group in which considerable human development takes place. How the child is valued and treated by the parents helps shape the child's view of the world as welcoming or hostile. Children's experiences begin to structure their thinking for future social interactions. Gradually, new agents of socialization emerge, including peer groups, church, and the school. To understand the significance of each of these agents of socialization, it is necessary to understand how they fit or interact with one another and to also understand the cognitive and affective development of the individual. This developmental process suggests the importance of framing the learning and practice of social behavior as civic careers. Furthermore, civic careers span time and a variety of social contexts, with each context having the possibility of influencing the next context. Therefore, to understand why individuals engage themselves in voluntary behaviors, it is necessary to explore the dynamic life history of the individual.

CONCLUSION

The purpose of this book is to identify ways in which social institutions can promote active engagement in the various voluntary associations within civil society. Most research in political socialization focuses on national or state politics or service outside of one's local community. This precludes explorations of how and why individuals first become involved in civil society, since civic involvement generally begins in more immediate or intimate associations. Furthermore, it is not only necessary to focus on a communal context in which primary and secondary groups influence norms of collective behavior, but it is also necessary to explore why people get involved rather than why they do not. This approach is more likely to yield descriptions of the experiences and the influences of the agents of socialization that first lead to involvement in civil society. The key agents of socialization that have been discussed in this chapter include family, church, peers, education, media, work, and the voluntary associations themselves. As argued throughout this chapter, these agents of socialization influence the "knowledge, skills, beliefs, values, attitudes, and dispositions" (Stacey, 1977, p. 2) that guide subsequent behavior, including participation in civil society. More specifically, this book focuses on the values, norms, motivations, and beliefs regarding community life that lead to direct involvement in voluntary associations and enlightened self-interest; it also explores how these aspects of human behavior are generated by the various agents of socialization.

Chapter 4

Researching Engaged Citizens in Civil Society

This book attempts to describe and understand a particular form of citizenship that includes both active engagement in civil society and enlightened self-interest. Enlightened self-interest is the ability of citizens to understand their private interests within a larger public context (Tussman, 1997). Putnam (1993) and others (Barber, 1995; Bellah et al., 1985) argue that enlightened self-interest comes from active engagement in the various voluntary associations that comprise civil society. However, whether or not this is true is irrelevant if citizens do not choose to get involved in civil society in the first place. By examining citizens who model, by reputation and by deed, this particular form of citizenship, it may be possible to understand how these individuals came to be involved in such citizenship and to better learn how to promote such involvement.

To find examples of such models of citizenship, one must focus on a particular community. A community provides the context in which active civic behavior can be identified and understood. A community has knowledge of its members and their contributions to civic life; it also has specific norms of civic behavior that are both recognized and acknowledged to be acceptable to the community and that lead to some common good. By exploring a single community, it is also possible to come to a practical understanding of which kinds of organizations contribute to the well-being of the community and the role citizens play in maintaining these organizations.

Focusing on a particular community is also critical to understanding how its normative structures and practices influence participation in civil society and the promotion of enlightened self-interest. By interviewing active members within the same community, it is possible to identify patterns of civil society that lead to enlightened self-interest and to discern if enlightened self-interest is preliminary to participation in the various voluntary associations that make up civil society.

COMMUNITY SITE SELECTION

In choosing a single community or case study approach, a typical middle-class community was found that represented where the majority of the United States population is raised. Studying such a community would provide important information about understanding how communities socialize citizens to participate in civil society and to see how these citizen models influence young people today.

According to Scott (1990), 77 percent of all U.S. citizens are raised and live in metropolitan areas. The U.S. Census (1992) indicates that most people in metropolitan areas live outside of the central city. These areas are what the U.S. Census (1992) refers to as the "central place" and the "outer urban fringe." Scott (1990) also found that 50 percent of Americans said that small towns are the best places for raising children, and that they would prefer to live in such places. Given this information, it was decided to find what the census defines as a typical "urban fringe area."

Other criteria for site selection had to do with access to the community. To have contacts in the community, and to have some knowledge of its history, was an important condition to gain the trust of the interviewees. Therefore, the Town of Bedford was chosen, because this site fit the description of a typical American urban fringe community, at least in the Northeast United States, and the researcher had contacts already established in the community.[1]

RESEARCH APPROACH

To take up the question of how model citizens came to be engaged in the voluntary associations that make up their community required a more complex understanding than was possible due to the limited research available. Most research on citizenship is focused on voting behavior, or on those acts that are directly related to public policy. This research is interested in how citizens become engaged in the resolution of public problems on a local level. The resolution of public problems may include local municipal government, but it also includes the communal associations that make up the community. These indigenous associations and their ability to resolve "grassroots" problems resemble the America that deTocqueville described in the mid-1800s. These communal groups rely on the initiative and commitment of local citizens to resolve problems and to provide for the common good of the community.

Since the research in this area was limited, and since the complexity of the socialization process was so great, it was decided to take a qualitative approach involving the life histories of local community activists. The life history approach requires that the researcher "conducts extensive interviews with one person for the purpose of collecting a first-person narrative" (Bogdan & Biklen, 1992, p. 64). This method is well suited to case study research, and—when used as a sociological or psychological approach to studying individuals—the life history method typically organizes data collection and presentation as a life course or "career" (Bogdan & Biklen, 1992, p. 65). "Sociological life histories often try to construct subjects' careers by emphasizing the role of organizations, crucial events, and significant others in shaping subjects' evolving definitions of self and their perspectives on life" (Bogdan & Biklen, 1992, p. 65). This life course or career approach best reflects the complexity of political socialization and allows for the emergence of new explanations in understanding the development of enlightened self-interest and engagement in civil society.

SUBJECT SELECTION

Selecting subjects for these life histories involved a three-stage process. The rationale behind the process of selecting subjects was to identify them by their reputations in this particular community, the Town of Bedford. This reputational approach was based on the work of Floyd Hunter (1963).

The first stage of the process was to identify model citizens through random telephone calls to residents within the Town of Bedford. These calls, conducted during October 1995, identified voluntary associations and individuals living in the town who contributed to the welfare of the town. While this technique did result in identifying organizations, only one person was willing to provide names of individuals who fit the description of "model citizen."

Selecting residents to call in this first stage began by obtaining property records from the town government. Businesses were eliminated, and residences were separated from undeveloped lots based on the property price (e.g., a record with an assessed value at $30,000 was most likely just a lot). Once a residence was identified, the address was confirmed by checking the telephone book. The list was randomized by assigning numbers to each record and then choosing these numbers from a book of random numbers (Gay, 1996, p. 602). Phone calls were made to these homes once an advertisement had been placed in the local paper explaining the research project.

After several telephone calls, it became evident that the residents in the Town of Bedford identified with either the northern part of the Town of

Bedford and the Village of Bedford Spa or the southern part of Bedford and the Village of Thomas Hills. Since the research was to focus on one community, the southern village was chosen, because it was determined to be more representative of an urban fringe area (i.e., it was closer to the central city area). This was also the area where the researcher had already established the most contacts.

The population of the Town of Bedford is approximately 8,073 residents, according to the 1990 census. Excluding the northern part of the town or the Village of Bedford Spa, there were close to 2,000 households. This list of households was randomized, as mentioned earlier, and calls were made based on this list. After calling fifty or so households, information became redundant; organizations were repeatedly referred to. These organizations included the volunteer ambulance squad, the fire department, the Human Services Center (HSC), the zoning board, the planning board, the Rotary Club, the Bedford Lake Improvement Association, Saint Mary's Catholic Church, Lucas Elementary School, the Women's Auxiliary, 4-H, and the Parent-Teacher Association. During these calls, most respondents refused to provide the names of individuals, so the focus was solely on organizations. Full descriptions of interview questions are provided in appendix A.

The next step was to contact organizations and set up interviews with organizational representatives. Typically these representatives were leaders of their organizations or handled the public relations for their group. The following people were interviewed in November 1995: Rotary (current president), fire department (social coordinator), ambulance (director), Methodist church (minister), Catholic church (priest), HSC (director), school board (principal and chair of school board), the town clerk, and the mayor (zoning and planning boards). The organizations selected were based on the frequency of mention according to the random phone survey. Organizations that did not operate within the Village of Thomas Hills were eliminated.

The interviews involved meeting these organizational representatives face-to-face and were conducted in order to identify subjects for study. The interviews were not taped, but notes were kept, and the interview was written up immediately afterward. During these interviews, the group representatives were asked questions about their organizations. They were also asked about individuals within their group who were actively committed to the organization and community, and who fit the citizen model of enlightened self-interest (see appendix B for interview schedule).

These face-to-face interviews with nine leaders of the significant voluntary associations in the community yielded a list of forty people. The list of potential subjects was stratified by age and gender to get a more even balance of respondents (eleven women and twenty-nine men were in the original list). Age was more difficult to ascertain, but through previously established contacts, the researcher knew the ages of several of the subjects. One of the organizational representatives mentioned that there were few, if any, people who were active in the community younger than thirty years of age. This seemed to be true of the subjects who were identified by these nine leaders as the model citizens described earlier. Out of the list of forty community notables, twelve men and eight women were chosen for the study. Beyond stratifying the original list by age and gender, subject selection was arbitrary. On the final subject list, there were nine males and two females born between 1918 and 1940, and four males and five females born between 1943 and 1957.

Of the twenty subjects originally selected for study, all but one were interviewed. A convenient time for interviewing this last subject never occurred during the period the interviews were conducted. Subjects were interviewed in their homes or at the office of their respective voluntary associations. The interviews, conducted in January and February 1996, were taped and usually lasted from two to three and a half hours (see appendix C for interview schedule). All interviewees were asked to sign an authorization form approved by Syracuse University (see appendix E). A brief biography on the subjects is provided in appendix D.

The table that follows provides a list of names, ages, job titles, education, and affiliations with community voluntary associations of each of the nineteen subjects interviewed. The names and titles of the community voluntary associations have been altered to protect the identity of the subjects and the community.

The organizational leaders of the more significant voluntary organizations in the Town of Bedford identified all of these individuals. These leaders or organizational representatives were asked if they could identify individuals within their organization who "contribute a lot of time and energy to volunteer efforts in their community, who are aware of local news and issues, and who are able to keep their own self-interest with a broader public context" (see appendix B). Many of these individuals were mentioned by more than one person. This supports the point made by Verba, Schlozman, and Brady (1995), that individuals are often recruited from one organization into another.

Art Forbes was the oldest of all of the subjects. He had been raised in the area, and except for the time he went to college, he has always lived here. He was able to describe some of the history of the town and how it grew. I interviewed him on his seventy-eighth birthday. He had retired several years ago and turned his veterinarian business over to two of his sons. His background in agriculture and his business kept him involved with many of the farmers in the area. He had initiated an agricultural assessment that allowed farmers to reduce their property taxes. He had also been one of the founding members of the town's Rotary Club. The current president of the Rotary Club said that its mission is to support the people and the activities of the community. The club

TABLE 1
SELECTED INFORMATION ON SUBJECTS (ORDERED BY BIRTH YEAR)

Name	Birth Year	Employment	Education	Affiliations
Art Forbes	1918	Veterinarian	Veterinarian school	Rotary
Frank Michaels	1919	School principal	BS	HSC, Girls School
Charles Witt	1926	Engineer	BS, MS	HSC, school board, library board
Peter Driscoll	1927	Engineer	BS, MS	School board, church, sports programs
Roger Smith	1927	Manager	BS	Methodist church, Rotary, HSC
Anne Sharpe	1928	Teacher/Housewife	BS, MA	School board, HSC
Chuck Wallace	1928	Engineering/HR manager	BS, MS	Methodist church
James Rockford	1930	Consulting/ Woodworking business	BS	Planning board
Phyllis Constantino	1938	Catholic Family Services	Nursing school	Catholic church
Mike Conners	1940	Teacher	BA	Methodist church, former fireman
Terry Nicols	1943	Housewife	BA	School board, Women's Club, BOCES president
Mary Hedberg	1946	Optometrist	BS, MS	Catholic church
Kathy Madison	1950	Teacher	BA, MA	Methodist church
Andrea Califano	1951	Teacher	BS	Catholic church
Jan Hyland	1951	School guidance	BA, MA	Methodist church
Linda Simmons	1952	Marketing	AA	Parks and recreation, Assessment Review Board
Chester Adams	1955	Community college teacher	BS	Ambulance squad
Todd Bueller	1956	Manufacturing	High school	Fire department
Oscar Thomas	1957	State employment agency	BA, MA	School board

has four avenues of service: vocation, community, club, and international. Forbes's other work in the community included serving on the board of the Lancaster Girls School, a private, not-for-profit school for delinquent youth.

Another subject whose job tied him to the community was *Frank Michaels*. Michaels had been the principal of the high school. In his job, he was able to learn firsthand about the needs of the community, especially its young people. This knowledge led him to help create the Human Services Center, a nongovernment agency that looks after the needs of the youth in the community. After his retirement, he was elected town supervisor and served on the county board of supervisors and the county planning board. He has also served on the board of the Lancaster Girls School.

Many of these subjects had been involved with the schools, particularly on the school board. *Charles Witt* had been on the school board for thirteen years. He became involved with it because he was concerned about education and volunteered to serve on a committee focusing on school budget issues. While serving on the committee, he found other people who were equally concerned about education. He decided to continue to work on educational issues by serving on the school board. He left when he began to feel that he saw his position as a right. He said:

> I recognized that, when I was the senior member in terms of service on the school board, I began to feel and recognize that I felt almost an ownership to which I had a right. Then I knew it was time to leave.

At the time of the interview, Witt was the current president of the Human Services Center and was serving on the local library board.

Peter Driscoll has served on the school board longer than anyone—twenty years. He began when his children were younger and continues to serve even today after retirement. He believes that "you'd like to leave this world better than when you entered it." He also is very involved in the state school board association and travels quite a bit for it. He has been involved in athletic programs for the communities' youth and is an active member in the service and social programs in his church.

Roger Smith was identified by several people, but the minister of his church seemed to sum it up best when he said that Smith "provides a good experience of what we ought to be doing, a lot of the time." He is involved in Rotary, the Human Services Center, and his church. When there was a flood in the Midwest, he helped organize some members of the community to go there to help. Smith was one of the more difficult subjects to interview. He did not talk about himself unless asked for specific personal information, and even then he did not say very much.

Anne Sharpe is another member of the school board but has done substantial work with the Human Services Center as well. Perhaps due to her own childhood relations with her parents, particularly her father, she does a lot of work with parenting support. She works very hard to create programs for troubled teens and to help busy parents make the most of their family life.

Chuck Wallace, like many of the subjects, was mentioned by more than one organizational leader in the community. He was involved in the Methodist church, Boy Scouts, a local conference on youth, the town council, and Rotary. The current president of Rotary (offices within the organization are rotated on a regular basis) said, "whatever he [Chuck] is involved in, he's really out there in front."

The town supervisor identified *James Rockford*, who is the current chair of the town planning board. Rockford moved into the area with his family when the community was growing, roughly between 1946 and 1957. With this growth, Rockford and his wife observed "other people doing things." They felt that they needed to get involved as well; it was "the responsible thing to do," or "the right thing to do." They became involved in the Parent-Teacher Association (PTA), the Methodist church, the local YMCA, Indian Guides (a program for young children), Little Troy Park, and the part of the Republican Party "that takes an active interest . . . on a town basis." Rockford said that "people ought to be contributing; we can't just be takers."

Phyllis Constantino was one of a few of these subjects whose work life was related to volunteerism. The priest in the local Catholic church identified her. Constantino works for Catholic Family Services and has used that position to get involved, on a voluntary basis, in a variety of places such as Habitat for Humanity and the local food pantry, and she also does work to inform the community about a variety of local and regional problems. Her church and the people she has met there have encouraged much of her involvement. One priest in particular taught her to take more "ownership" of the problems of the community. She said that she is "deeply entrenched in my faith journey, and connecting that with my family and with service to my community and my church."

The current Rotary president identified *Mike Conners* as someone "extremely involved in his church and in his community as well as Rotary." Conners teaches in one of the local elementary schools and has always "loved working with people." He had been a local voluntary fireman and a trustee in his church, and he teaches adult education courses at the Human Services Center. His involvement with Rotary was based on its traditions of service to the community. He feels that "the community needs people to assist."

The principal of the local high school identified *Terry Nicols*, who has been involved with the school board for a number of years. Nicols is also involved with the BOCES program (a vocational program for teenagers) and the

Women's Club. While she has worked as a social worker and recreational therapist, she stopped work when she had children, which led to her community involvement. "Some of the things I was involved in I became involved in through them [her children], as I think most mothers do when you see a need. You have the opportunity to help, so you go do it." She has also seen her volunteering as personal growth. She said:

> When you get involved in the kinds of things I've done, you have opportunities to take courses, to go to workshops, to go to conventions, and you learn not only what you need to know to help the organization you're involved in, but you learn things that help you to grow.

The priest at the local Catholic church also mentioned *Mary Hedberg*. Her involvement is similar to Nicols in that she sees her involvement as growth oriented, but her underlying motivation for involvement is more similar to the "town father" ideal discussed by Bellah et al. (1985). Hedberg is active in the church, but her involvement beyond it is much greater. Through the Rotary, she works with an alternative sentencing program. She has been the democratic chairperson for the town, has served on the Human Services Center Board, and has been involved in many of the local organizations designed to support and encourage business growth in the area. This includes the county chamber of commerce, the County Leadership Program, the Business Professional Association for the Town of Bedford (president), and the Counties Economic and Business Promotion Committee. She is also involved in numerous professional groups associated with optometry. Her promotion of her own business and her efforts to promote business in the town and for the county reflect an understanding that her business will be more profitable if the community is healthy—economically and politically.

The minister of the local Methodist church identified *Kathy Madison*. He said of her, "she has a lot of courage. She takes stands against the status quo. This needs to happen. She always has ideas of what can be done." Most of Madison's work has been as the head of the Out Reach Commission in the church. This group helps raise money for a variety of organizations, including the Human Services Center, the City Mission, and other causes. The group also tries to raise awareness. Madison feels that it is important to make the community aware of those in need and to encourage them to help. She feels that many people in the community cannot commit too much because of their busy lives, but that they still "feel a need to do something." She helps facilitate this by producing a booklet on "Community Volunteering Opportunities."

The priest of the Catholic church also identified *Andrea Califano*. Her involvement, like that of Constantino, Sharpe, and Hyland, is tied more to spiritual growth. Califano's parents had instilled in her that "your faith and your church has a lot to do with who you are and what you are . . . because of that I wanted to get involved." She works for a group called St. Vincent DePaul in her church, which helps people in need on an emergency basis (i.e., food, rent, and power bills) or with problems of domestic violence. Califano also works with another church and another group, both of which help provide food to the needy of a nearby town.

Jan Hyland also fits the description of someone who ties spirituality to community commitment. She has been in "80 percent of the possible jobs" in her church, including fund-raising, advocacy for the poor, education, staff/parish relations, choir, and even preaching. She is also involved with groups or associations tied to her children's activities, including drama, sports, and the PTA. The minister of the Methodist church said that Hyland was someone "who really challenges us to identify people and to meet their needs. She has a lot of love and energy." Hyland says that she needs to "believe a purpose beyond myself, not just the day-to-day, hand-to-mouth kind of living or just accumulating things."

Linda Simmons serves as a good example of how self-interest grows into enlightened self-interest. She had helped organize the community around some concerns over development in her neighborhood; a large development was threatening the water and traffic capacities of the town. Her skills in working to keep this development from going forward without addressing these concerns and her willingness to get involved in the community led to her appointment to the Parks and Recreation Committee and the Grievance Day Committee, both unpaid volunteer positions appointed by the town supervisor. As she put it, "being one of the larger mouths in that group, they remembered me and said you know we're trying to get this group together and would you be interested in being on this committee." Like others who have children, Simmons was also involved in the PTA and in some organizations associated with her children's activities.

Unlike some of the other subjects, *Chester Adams* and *Todd Bueller* were both involved with singular organizations that dominated their involvement in the community. Both of them worked for voluntary emergency services organizations—Adams with Bedford Emergency Services and Bueller with the Bedford Lake Fire Department.

Adams had been involved in emergency-type services since he was in high school. He began as a lifeguard and then started to volunteer with the ambulance squad. He went on to receive paramedic training and actually teaches paramedic work for a living. The head of the local squad said that Adam's "attitude, conduct, performance, duties, and intuition" make him the kind of person I was looking for. Many people who Adams knew as professionally paid paramedics could not understand why he volunteered so much of his time to the community. Adams said that "maybe I do a little more than some others, but I think most of the people I associate with do some kind of activity."

Bueller is the local chief of the fire department, a very demanding position due to the increasing regulation of volunteer fire companies. His involvement was greatly influenced by his ties to the community—he grew up here—and his brothers' involvement. They all joined the fire department as soon as they were eighteen years old. At the time, the fire department provided a lot of social activities for its members. Today, however, that has changed. Bueller said:

> I still get enjoyment out of it, but it's not fun anymore. I guess the reason I'm doing it more now is because someone's got to do it. . . . Someone's got to be here if a house is burning and there is somebody trapped inside or somebody injured.

Oscar Thomas was the last subject interviewed for this book. The local Catholic priest identified him for his work on social justice issues and his work on the school board. His involvement seemed to be a confluence of events, both past and present. The most engaging was the connection of his family life with national events. He said:

> The other thing that impacted me was interesting. The full buildup to the Persian Gulf War was then only a few months old. Margaret [his wife] called me up at work and said, "Ben [his son] just doesn't look good, I think he is having a hard time breathing, I'm going to take him to the hospital." So I immediately left the office and drove home, and as I was driving home and thinking about this little kid, two months old, and I was just realizing how precious his life is. And thinking about this buildup and that we were going to turn Iraq into a parking lot by carpet-bombing them into submission, realizing that innocent people were going to get killed and maimed, and thinking about this two-month-old kid who was going to the hospital and who knows what's wrong with him and putting the two together. You know life is so precious for me as the parent of a two-month-old kid. Isn't life as precious for two-month-old kids in Iraq or Kuwait or wherever we were thinking about carpet-bombing? And it was after that point, when I really started the vigil . . . about the war. It was just so obvious to me that this is no way to deal with the situation.

Thomas's vigil led him to think more deeply about how he could make a difference. His own work was based around love of career development and "helping people find their niche and find their way." He began to become interested "in assisting other people through my impact on systems," particularly by serving on the school board.

INTERVIEWS

As seen by these brief overviews of the subjects, their comments varied widely in their citizen involvement, their motivations, and the history of their connections to the community. Some subjects were more able to talk about their life histories at length with little prompting, while others seemed to respond only to direct questions. Some interviews lasted much longer than others, because some subjects presented more descriptive data and/or presented lengthier stories. Overall, the subjects were very willing to discuss their lives in a surprisingly candid manner. They were also willing to give up several hours to discuss their experiences growing up and their roles within the community. (A brief biography of some of the major influences and events in the lives of these subjects is presented in appendix D.)

The objectives of the interviewing process were twofold. First, a description of these model citizens was necessary. This would provide possible outcome variables for the construction of programs and experiences that might be created to promote engagement in civil society. Second, these interviews were intended to bring out the unique socialization processes that lead to these outcome variables.

INTERVIEW SCHEDULE

Political socialization as a field of study is substantial enough to provide many significant variables that are related to citizenship behavior and civil society. Therefore, the use of an interview schedule seemed appropriate in this research on socialization to civil society (Bogdan & Biklen, 1992, p. 77). This made it possible to explore the agents of socialization as well as other key variables related to involvement in voluntary associations, mentioned in the earlier chapters. Interview schedules "generally allow for open-ended responses and are flexible enough for the observer to note and collect data on unexpected dimensions of the topic" (Bodgan & Biklen, 1992, p. 77).

The interview schedule (see appendix C) began with general questions designed to examine how the subjects described themselves, their community, and their affiliations with the community. The schedule was modeled partially on O'Neill's (1981) work, "Cognitive Community Psychology." The questions used elicited responses that described the subjects in terms of their personal values, norms, and motivations and their beliefs about the civic life of the community.

The second part of the interview schedule was designed to explore issues of socialization and the "civic careers" of the subjects. They were asked questions about family, parents, peers, school, and the communities in which they grew up, as well as the communities in which they currently live, attend church, and work. These questions provided a life history of the individual and offered insight into how the several socialization agents worked together over time for each subject.

Lastly, several questions were asked that addressed the issues of age cohort and life course development. (For a complete list of questions and expectations of responses, see sppendix C.)

ANALYSES OF INTERVIEWS

Each interview was transcribed to a digital format, which provided the basis for analytic induction (Bogdan & Biklen, 1992). Analytic induction is a qualitative approach to analyze data and to synthesize theories. It focuses on several cases of particular phenomena to determine patterns of behavior. For this research, the cases or subjects were specific individuals who represented an ideal model of citizenship. One advantage of this qualitative approach is that it encourages the use of open interview schedules. This is important because in the past political socialization literature relied heavily on fixed-choice questions and answers (Renshon, 1977). This has inhibited understanding of what can be a dynamic socialization process (see Coles, 1987).

Data analysis was supported through the use of a computer program, Ethnograph (Seidel, Friese, & Leonard, 1995). It allowed for coding and the comparative analysis of codes across subjects (Strauss, 1987). This comparison helped generate nonrandom themes or patterns in the data. Themes are "some signal trend, some master conception, or key distinction" (Mills, 1959, p. 216). For this study, themes or patterns of responses were identified when three or more respondents had similar descriptions, responses, or experiences. Exceptions to this rule are mentioned, and these exceptions are identified when the subjects' responses contained powerfully explanatory affect. The development of these citizenship themes allowed for further comparisons between this study and others within the field of political socialization.

DESIGN STATEMENT

Socialization to civil society is important in that civil society is critical to the creation of social capital and to the mediation of degenerative forms of individualism. Social capital encourages the collective action of citizens in the proper functioning of democratic institutions and to the resolution of public problems. Such civic involvement also depends on and promotes enlightened self-interest, balancing the influences of the media and the market, which can lead to economic and social wilding. Therefore, it becomes important to promote the involvement of good citizenship in civil society, particularly the voluntary associations that teach the norms and values of collective action and that help promote the civic capacity of enlightened self-interest.

Research on how and why people choose to become involved in the voluntary associations of civil society is limited. Most of this research is concerned with political society and civic behavior related to electoral politics. The research that does speak to issues of involvement in voluntary associations tends to focus on noncommunal forms of civic action and lacks descriptive detail in answering the question of how we can promote civic engagement in civil society through various mediating institutions. Communal contexts are important in understanding citizenship in that individuals first learn the norms of collective action in these more immediate primary and secondary groups. These norms are also influenced along with many other important determinants of social behavior through other agents of socialization. These agents include childhood influences such as neighborhood or community life, family, church, peers, education, and organizational involvement, and adult influences, such as historical events, family of procreation, work, community life, and organizational involvement. Together these agents influence the values, norms, motivations, and beliefs regarding community life and public problem solving.

To understand how these agents influence citizen behavior in regard to voluntary associations of community life, it is necessary to identify those individuals who are currently involved in their communities and who exemplify enlightened self-interest. Since this is not easily identified outside of a community context in which people are knowledgeable about one another, and since the focus here is on the more immediate influence of primary and secondary groups, a community study approach was necessary. This helped identify model citizens through reputational sampling. Furthermore, a community study provides a context in which civic behavior can be understood.

This book identifies individuals in this one community who fit this ideal model of citizenship. Of course, they have been identified by their involvement in the various voluntary associations identified in this community and by their reputations. However, these are inadequate in understanding what causes these individuals to act in the ways they do. Values, virtues and/or norms, motivations, and belief systems determine behavior. Therefore, in chapter 5, the book develops patterns of these behavioral determinants across all of our subjects. These determinants are largely the result of social learning that occurs through socialization.

The main focus of this research is really to understand the patterns of socialization that lead to these determinants. What agents of socialization lead to the values, norms, motivations, and belief systems that foster engagement in civic life and participation in the numerous voluntary associations critical to the life of a community? Chapter 6 provides those answers. Again, by looking across all nineteen subjects, patterns or themes emerge that suggest how certain agents and experiences influence how individuals practice citizenship in their communities. A life history approach was used to generate these patterns or themes.

In the concluding chapter 7, these patterns of socialization will be discussed in the context of previous findings regarding these many agents of socialization. As mentioned in chapter 3, however, these previous findings are rarely related directly to the work done here. Often the focus of these earlier works tried to understand socialization to different aspects of citizenship, particularly civic behavior that attempts to directly influence state government. Chapter 7 will also provide some suggestions for how some of the more significant agents of socialization can work to promote citizen involvement in voluntary associations that promote community welfare. In discussing these suggestions, it will be clear that this book is a first step. Chapter 7 concludes by stating some of the limitations of this study and what further research needs to be done.

Certainly the hope of this work is that more attention will be paid to how we generate the ideal models that we have found through our subject selection, subjects who demonstrate commitment to their communities through their work and who demonstrate a form of self-interest properly contextualized within a broader social structure of community. To promote such citizenship, we may need to rethink the practices of our social institutions or—at the very least—become more aware of what they already do well to promote social responsibility. But before that can begin, it is necessary to first describe what it is about these individuals that causes them to act publicly through enlightened self-interest.

Chapter 5

Citizen Models for Civil Society

This book identifies nineteen subjects who represent an ideal model of citizenship. These individuals commit large amounts of time and energy to a number of voluntary associations that contribute to the community. These people are known to place their own self-interest within a broader context of public life; they act from what Tussman (1997) calls "enlightened self-interest." Within a community, the presence of these types of ideal citizens assures the success of the mediating structures within civil society, promotes the possibilities of collective action, and counteracts the influence of excessive individualism.

The central question of this book is how to promote the development of such ideal citizenship. However, before we can understand why these individuals act as model citizens, we need to know more about them. If we wish to explore the process of how they came to be the citizens that they have become, then we need to fully describe them and the underlying qualities that cause them to act as they do.

The need to understand why these individuals act as they do was an important objective of the interviews. Subjects were asked to describe themselves and to explain why they are involved in the voluntary associations of civil society. An analysis of all subject responses generated patterns or themes that can be used to provide a general description of these model citizens. These patterns comprised four categories, including values, virtues or norms, beliefs about public life and community, and motivations. Chapter 5 will examine each of these categories and how they describe the subjects in this study. In chapter 6, how the various agents of socialization led to the development of these characteristics in these subjects will be explored.

VALUES

Subjects' value systems were among the first categories that emerged from the interview process. Values are "shared ideas about what is socially desirable" (Thompson & Hickey, 1994, p. 72). In a sense, values are those aspects of social life that we try to acquire or emulate. The subjects in this research most often mentioned that they valued people, education and learning, and family life over materialistic gain.

Family over Materialism

The valuing of family and family life, often referred to in juxtaposition to materialism, was a dominant theme among the participants in this research. Subjects made life choices by deciding between those options that benefited family life and those that led to material wealth. The subjects and the parents of the subjects in this book tended to choose options that benefited family and family life. Since family is the "primary social institution" (Gillespie & Allport, as cited in Hyman, 1959, p. 69), it may be argued that an individual's family experience influences children's dispositions toward others (Daloz et al., 1996, p. 27), and how he or she values other social institutions.

Thus if the family members, in the first experience of civil society, value time together, pay attention to one another, and care for one another, then a child raised in such a family gains personal satisfaction through primary groups. This satisfaction may lead to valuing group interaction, and in the future the child is more likely to choose to be involved in the other mediating institutions of civil society (i.e., school, church, sports, clubs, etc.).

Furthermore, many of the subjects' first pull toward involvement in the larger, more public institutions of civil society began with their commitment to their children. They became involved in the PTA of their children's schools or the clubs and sporting groups to which their children belonged. Often, an involvement of this kind—just beyond but still connected to the institution of family—is a beginning point for future involvement, as will be explained in chapter 6.

The valuing of family life over material wealth was also present across the different generations of these subjects, despite their very different historical circumstances. Two of the most significant events affecting circumstances for the older subjects in this research were the Great Depression of the early 1930s and World War II. Families who lived during these periods had few expectations to possess material goods. However, the family did provide a relatively stable source for the basic needs, which included a sense of being "cared for."

You didn't have a lot of money, you didn't ask for a lot of money, you didn't assume you were going to get a lot of money, but we had enough. (Rockford)

I really didn't think too much of it at the time, but looking back at it, I can see, that, yeah, we were deprived in a way. But I think that we had each other. And so we had a close relationship—the kids in the family. (Conners)

You knew you didn't have a lot of money, but there was a lot of pride, a lot of caring. (Wallace)

The subjects in this research of the World War II generation and the baby boom generation[1] both valued stable and committed marriages, along with the valuing of family life. Forbes, born in 1918, proudly mentioned that he has been married fifty-four years. Bueller, born in 1956, also was proud of his commitment to his marriage and saw his relationship with his wife as an example to his children. "What I have realized is that you can be a skilled parent, but if you don't have a good relationship within the family with a spouse, you don't set a very good foundation and role model for the kids."

Although some participants from the baby boom generation mentioned similar values and expectations of choosing family life over material goods, a few also saw different patterns emerging. Califano (born in 1950) pointed out that many of today's families prioritize material goods over spending time with their loved ones.

Well, I think a lot of people today feel, and I think it is too bad, that they can't live on one income . . . I honestly believe you can learn to live with what you have, if you really, really want to. I think what happens very often is you get two-income families and, the more you have, the more you want. . . . I'm very content, I've always been very content. (Califano)

Hyland believes that the "flip side" of living in an affluent community is that "people are really struggling to kind of bring in more income to have more things then—maybe there isn't the time to supervise [the children]." Of course, for many working-class American families, one income does not go far enough. Even when they have two incomes, many families can barely afford food, shelter, and medical care, much less unnecessary goods or services.

Across generations, the subjects in this book share a value of and personal satisfaction with family life, rather than a value of increasing opportunities for material gain. Unfortunately, some of the subjects felt that this focus on family life was in decline. If this is true, it is unfortunate, as the value of family life over material wealth may be critical to mediate the influence of the market on the values of children. Today, children's sense of self-worth is too often based on access to and ability to demonstrate command of material possessions. The emphasis on material identity has even lead to brutal incivility: children commit violence over the possession of expensive clothes.

People

Perhaps related to early support in family life, another value that emerged as being important to the subjects in this research was to be with or part of a group of people. These subjects were highly social in nature. They "liked to work with others" (Madison) and had a "need to socialize" (Wallace). For many of the subjects, it was a matter of being known and of having a shared history in a community. Rockford stated:

> Well, it's nice to run into people you have been involved in with various activities and say, "hi, how are you," and "didn't we have good times with that program and this program," or "I haven't seen you since we did this or that." You find the people you have known over the years are a part of that group who are still involved to some degree in something.

Others, like Hyland, felt a connection with other community members through shared notions of belief. "I need that connection. Not necessarily with a specific church, but I need a connection with a body of people who believe in something greater than themselves . . . who believe in God."

For both of these subjects, there is an underlying value in being with others with whom certain beliefs and experiences are shared. This value of a common or shared life is fundamental to civic life and is the basis on which public problem solving must take place. When problems and disagreements do develop in a mutually recognized, associative community, one is more concerned with reacting in a manner that both parties deem appropriate to the situation: one reacts with civility.

The need to be connected to others is also one of the motivations that led to involvement in voluntary associations. As will be explained later in this chapter, the need for social gratification is one of the most fundamental and more frequently mentioned motivations for involvement in the voluntary associations of civil society.

Education

Education, the ability to read, and lifelong learning were also highly valued by the subjects in this research. Many subjects grew up in families that valued education in spite of or due to the fact that the subjects' parents had limited education. "Education was valued in my household, at least in part, because my parents never had the opportunity" (Nicols). Even those subjects who did not continue with their formal education wanted to ensure that their children would go on to college.

> What I am going to do is to try the best I can to be able to encourage my children [to] go ahead and pursue further education, because I think, [in] this day and age, you almost have to if you are going to be able to survive financially, so I'm really going to encourage them to go to school. (Bueller)

Bueller went on to mention the cost of higher education and how he and his wife were saving to put their children through college. It was interesting to see that many of the subjects in this study, particularly the men, were able to go on to college because of the GI bill, or scholarships of one kind or another. This suggests the value of state-supported higher education.

Education was of course seen as the means to provide economic opportunity through good jobs, but for many of these subjects, it was more than that. Education not only meant learning but also becoming better learners. The ability to learn helped these subjects to understand the issues of the day and to deal with the complexity of public life. Many, such as Witt and Rockford, also felt that their value of learning made it possible for them to be more open-minded individuals, an important characteristic that influenced how they dealt with public issues.

The value of openness is indeed an important aspect in the resolution of conflict. For the subjects in this research, openness meant the ability to genuinely listen to others in spite of any prejudicial feelings. It also meant that when one is trying to resolve public conflict, one needs to hear all sides before making up one's mind. According to these subjects, the ability to be open and to listen to others was a basic outcome of a good education.

VIRTUES AND NORMS

Along with values, there were a number of characteristics that related to how these citizens acted within their communities. It is difficult to qualify these characteristics as "virtues" or "norms." Novak (1995) describes virtues as "habits" or "settled dispositions or capacities" (p. 48). To be virtuous, one must be familiar with and act according to an accepted course prescribed by society. Norms are defined as "the rules, expectations, and guidelines that govern what people should or should not think, feel, or do in a given social situation" (Thompson & Hickey, 1994). Norms are the rules that dictate the accepted course of action, and virtues are the actions themselves. Typically someone is said to have virtue if she or he consistently acts according to certain norms or societal expectations for the roles she or he plays. The subjects in this research all had clear expectations of public behavior within their community and held themselves to these standards. Since there was a consistency of civic behavioral expectations across subjects, it is fair to say that these subjects are virtuous.

Subjects within Bekowtiz's (1987) *Local Heroes* also held certain virtues that were a key theme in his study. Berkowitz's subjects held a "belief in and reliance on traditional virtue" (1987, p. 323). These virtues were understood as a "composite of several different qualities" (ibid.), including:

> Commitment to the task at hand, and to the underlying cause.
> Hard work, plus the belief that hard work pays off.
> Persistence: a willingness to go over, around, or through obstacles; what we once called stick-to-it-iveness.
> Considerate treatment of others; practice of the Golden Rule.
> Riskiness, not necessarily in the entrepreneurial sense, but rather the readiness to take a chance.
> Tolerance for criticism, even for being called "crazy" by one's peers, as several participants independently reported.
> Belief in the power of a single person to affect larger events, even if self-esteem were low.
> Optimism that things will turn out well; there are very few pessimists here.

These virtues, or virtue "composites," like those found in this study, including self-reliance, perceiving and owning community need, competence, hard work or keeping busy, and honesty and civility, actually encourage action over inaction in the daily course of human life.

Self-Reliance

One consistent aspect for these subjects was an understanding of the importance of being self-reliant and not needing outside help. The idea of self-reliance is not related to individualism, however. Individualism serves as an end in itself, whereas self-reliance is a way of living one's life as an individual and as a member of a larger social group such as a family or community.

Thomas, a baby boomer, spoke about his need to look after himself within the family structure. As a child, he was diagnosed with diabetes. He said:

> I had to learn very young that I really had to rely on myself; I really had to take care of things. So as a very young kid, who had to start to watch my diet, take shots of insulin every day, had to basically manage this disease which was constant, you had to basically be conscious of it every single day of your life.

Thomas had to be sure that he took care of his own needs, and that he did not rely on other family members, particularly his mother, to help him out.

Many of the subjects saw themselves as having the ability and responsibility to act not only for their own benefit but also for the benefit of those social institutions to which they belong. Rockford talked about self-reliance and community life. He said:

> In all aspects I think there should be a high degree of self-reliance . . . the community should be self-reliant. When it can't do it then it goes to the next level of the community, be it the county or the state, and then as a last resort the federal government.

The idea that Rockford suggests here is one of subsidiarity, a political concept that will be explained further under the section in this chapter titled "Representation." Primarily, subsidiarity suggests that individuals must act within the various social institutions of which they are members. Citizens must assure the success of these institutions without outside help whenever possible. Self-reliance within civil society is an important virtue, because it promotes civic involvement in the many mediating institutions of civil society—family, neighborhood, community, town, and so on.

Perceiving and Owning Community Need

Communities can only be self-reliant when community members are aware of the needs of their neighbors and take on the responsibility for meeting those needs. In this study, it was clear that the participants were such citizens. When asked why she is volunteering so much of her time in the community, Sharpe says, "Why am involved in the community? I guess because I saw there was a need, and I wanted to do something about it." Bueller also has this quality. His involvement reflects an understanding of the safety needs of the community. When asked why he works for the volunteer fire department, Bueller says, "I guess the reason I'm doing it more now is because someone's got to do it. . . . Someone's got to be here if a house is burning and there's somebody trapped inside or somebody injured, somebody's got to be there to go ahead and provide assistance."

The subjects in this research not only saw the needs of the community, but they acted on them. For some, it was a matter of responsibility. "I think you also learn if kinda for every freedom you have there is incumbent responsibility" (Wallace). "I have been active in the community in many different ways. Both my wife and I, we have a strong feeling that that's the responsible thing to do" (Rockford). For others, this responsibility took the form of "ownership" of the situation. Constantino talked about how a local priest had encouraged a committee in her church to get started and how they "took own-ership" of their church's needs. She went on to describe ownership:

> Well, it means I guess that I really cannot just sit back to wait for things to happen. It means if anything is going to work that it is important that I do it, and if no one else does it, that's okay, but I can't wait for others to do it be-cause it might not happen.

Related to this practice of perceiving and owning the many needs of individu-als in the community is a sense of being able to do something about it. Each of the subjects in this research possessed a sense of competence and each felt that he or she were somewhat unique in what he or she could contribute to the wel-fare of the community.

Competence

> When I was asked to run for the school board, I guess there was a certain amount of ego involvement in this latter category that I have described, that, yeah, maybe there is something I could do differently as a member of the school board to make changes that would be for the better. (Witt)

Witt is an individual who believes that he can make a unique difference in the world. As stated earlier, the belief in having an ability to make a difference in the community is the result of a clear sense of competence. Competence, or the ability to do something well, is not only a virtue, it is also an essential self-belief for individuals to become engaged in community action. Verba, Schloz-man, and Brady (1995) argue that competency is a critical component of or key resource for civic volunteerism. Failure to perceive oneself as competent can lead to inaction and can make any involvement seem overwhelming. In fact, for many of the subjects in this research, recognition of competence by self or oth-ers was the beginning of involvement and social engagement. Subjects talked about how an earlier sense of competence builds on decisions for future actions and an even more enhanced sense of competence. All of the participants in this study had a strong sense of their abilities.

Hard Work and Keeping Busy

The general level of energy that these subjects demonstrated relates to this sense of competence. Many of the participants had full-time jobs and families with children, but they still managed to attend organizational meetings at night. Their obligations to these voluntary associations demanded time on weekends as well. When they talked about all of their responsibilities, it was clear that they believed in hard work and in keeping busy. Bueller explained how he became fire chief. "The chiefs before me worked just as hard. I think basically what happens is, if you were not committed you'd be filtered out before you reach that position.... One thing I know is if you're in the job, you got to give 100 percent."

Honesty and Civility

Other virtues that were frequently mentioned in this study dealt directly with politics. These virtues are honesty and civility. Many of the subjects considered the very act of politics uncivil. The participants in this research seemed to define politics as being elected to public positions that required the individuals elected to deal with uncivil constituents and dishonest money interests.

Smith said that he has not "wanted to get into politics." He explained further: "I guess I don't relish the rough and tumble." He explained rough and tumble as "dealing with unhappy constituents over sometimes trivial items." Forbes felt that he had enough to do running his own business, and that he didn't "want to go there and have somebody wrassle [*sic*] with me over some project, somebody wants to put a culvert in front of their house at twelve o'clock at night."

The subjects in this research also considered politics as a power issue revolving around party affiliation and money and entailing a loss of moral character on the part of the political participants. Wallace said:

> This is going to be a telling statement, but I'm too honest to be a politician. And I can't sell to the highest bidder, so I just have to stay out of it, because my wife says you'll be another Kennedy. You just can't be that open and straightforward, and that's my style.

Driscoll also felt that to get involved in politics meant being controlled by those who donate money. He said that he wanted to be independent. When I asked him if money meant being politically tied, he offered this explanation:

> Money, money would be, you know, political donation, like you find at the state level. This is just an example. A lot of money goes into the political pockets of politicians, and they in turn have got to respond to the people who donate the money. I don't want that, and I don't make decisions on politics, I make them for the kids. So I guess it's important to keep that clear of any politics.

Bueller felt that personal ties and reciprocity were more important than political ties, despite his father's wishes.

Politics don't interest me at all. Not whatsoever, none whatsoever. My father is the Democratic chairman for the Town of Bedford and stuff. He's a dedicated Democrat from start to finish. I'll give you an example. The town highway superintendent we have in the Town of the Bedford is Tom Clifton. He has done a lot for the fire department over the years. You know, we've gotten in a bind where we needed a bulldozer to pull the fire truck out of ditch, or we ran out of fuel . . . I mean the guy basically bends over backwards so when it comes time to vote in November my father will say, "Make sure you get out there and vote democrat." I tell him, "Dad I'm telling you right now I'm going to vote for the individual, I'm not going to vote straight democrat, that Tom Clifton." "Yeah, but you got to give these guys some opposition. If they go up there and win no contest every year, you got to have competition to keep him honest." So, I respect him for looking at it from that standpoint but it's hard for me to look at an individual whose helped me out as much as he has, when I go to the polls I vote for Cliff. So I guess political-wise I have my own beliefs . . . but I'm not much for politics as far as following politics.

This idea of not being political is also related to the value of openness. In two of the interviews conducted with the organizational representatives, the idea of "avoiding politics" came up. Avoidance was how the school board was able to resolve problems and be successful. Being nonpolitical referred to how one managed conflict and handled personal interests within a public setting. The norms for managing conflict, according to these two organizational representatives and to many of the subjects in this research, included being able "to listen and be open to others" and "being able to change one's opinion," given rational argument. Personal interests that tended to have a "single-issue focus" were rejected as an effective means to resolve public problems.

CONCEPTS AND BELIEFS
CONCERNING PUBLIC LIFE

In addition to the qualities and characteristics of the model citizens in this book, it is also important to understand how they think about public life. What does community mean to them? How do they go about resolving public problems in their community? What are their perceptions of how others solve community-related problems? Lastly, how do they think about their role in civil society? The answers to these questions provide a context for understanding how the subjects in this research choose to act. Their answers to these questions reveal what public life is like in this community, and why these particular subjects choose to become involved in the voluntary associations of this community.

Community Building

As mentioned before, the idea of "doing politics" or being "political" was not valued by these people. Smith talked about the difference between politics and "community building." To him, local politics, in terms of town government, has "never had any appeal." He tries to do "community building . . . in less spectacular ways." By community building, he refers to his work in Rotary. He said:

> For several years now, Rotary's had a Christmas tree over on the corner. We tried for many years to turn that into a community event where people would come and sing and so on. We never could pull it off until the last two years, but that's a community builder. I think of it as a sidewalk. Not a concrete sidewalk, but a social sidewalk that brings the community together.

What is striking is that the participants in this research do not see the political significance of their own involvement in their community. They see politics as what one does in office and their voluntary participation as something else. The views of the subjects in this research parallel some of the findings in a study done for the Kettering Foundation by the Harwood Group (1993), whose study focused on college students and their thoughts on politics and how they perceived their role in politics. The researchers found that students see politics as irrelevant, imagine a very different notion of politics, and do not learn to practice politics (Harwood Group, 1993, p. 2). This different "notion of politics" suggests a more local, community-based focus. In fact, as Levine (1993) points out, students tend to participate more directly in service to their communities. Students also see a more positive future for their communities, but not for the nation as a whole.

For both of these groups and for the American public as a whole, national politics, state politics, and, to some degree, local political offices are not where people want to put their energies.[2] They want to put them into places where they feel they can make a difference and not have to be corrupted by outside, noncommunity-related influences.

Community

The general questions asked during the interviews avoided using such words as "politics," "community," and "volunteerism," so that the subject's terminology could be revealed. This was not always possible when the participants in this research did not bring up any related terms. However, "community" came up quite frequently. The subjects defined "community" as knowing people or being known, by geography or where they lived, by shared interests or life situations, such as child rearing, and by economic benefit.

Community for some meant being known, and it seemed tied to the idea of primary groups, those one encounters in day-to-day contact. Community is a place where being known or knowing others is valued.

> We walk down the road in the summer, we see people that we know, and these are people, some of them senior citizens, some of them are people with kids like us, and some of them are new people that have just moved in. . . . Some of them are married couples; young married couples that have no children. It's almost like a little community, on this road. It's kind of nice. People say hello to one another all the time, even people at the end of the road that don't know us, way down there. (Thomas)

Nicols said:

> Community is place; community is people. . . . Your community is created by the accident of where you are. . . . It's an accident of geography and who happens to live on your street, whether they are in school with you, whether they have children when you have children, or they don't. So, place is pretty much choice or accident.

Those people who shared the raising of children and other interests created community through their interactions and knowledge of one another.

> People have a community interest, whether you are raising children at the same time, your children go to the same school, you belong to the same church, you have the same interests, you square dance together, you golf together. Whatever it is, you make your social choice, and that's choice based on interest. The ladies I paint with are my community, because we are roughly of an age within ten years. We all have children who are grown, so it's similar interests that create community. (Nicols)

The other notion of community for many of the subjects in this research related to economics. At some level community was a site in which the economic exchange of resources, ideas, or thinking was promoted. Conners said that human interaction was important. When asked why, he offered the following:

> People need it. . . . You need social interaction. You need to associate with other people. They can help you. You get better ideas if you have more people involved. But you sit at a meeting and somebody will get a germ of an idea, and you say, gee, I can add to that, you add something to it; somebody adds something to it, and when you get finished you have this product that no one person could do. But it's the product of everybody's collective thinking.

He also talked about communities as places where you could "pool resources." This was more of an economic benefit and involved each individual sharing her or his time and skills with others in the community. Conners said:

> Some people can do some things that other people can't do, and so some peo-
> ple are equipped physically to do something better than others. ... So ... you
> kind of pool your resources as well. It's not just the social, but the physical as-
> pects of it. Like somebody needs to have their driveway dug out or something
> like that, and yet they can do something for you that you might not necessar-
> ily like to do, or they may have a difficult time doing. So maybe it's the getting
> together of the physical aspects of it.

Conners paralleled this to "early communities with the trade goods, like one [person] became a blacksmith, one became a wheel smith, and together they became a community that helped each other." This is quite similar to the concept of general reciprocity, as mentioned in Putnam's (1993) work. One person helps another without immediate reward, knowing that sometime in the future the other will help if needed (Putnam, 1993).

This idea of community as an economic resource is discussed in Bellah et al.'s (1992) *The Good Society*. The authors cite John Snow (p. 261) and his proposition that in contemporary American society, "the bottom line of security is money, not extended family and community." Basically, Bellah et al. (1992) argue that people develop connections in communities that alleviate the economic costs of daily living. When someone lives in a community and develops long-term relationships, there can be more opportunities for the informal exchange of goods and services outside of the formal market. There is less opportunity for dishonest business practices as well, since individual reputations are communicated throughout the community. However, if one moves to a new community, these connections and the security they offer are lost.

Creating a Sense of Community

The subjects in this research were concerned about maintaining their community ties and relationships. One of the major objectives of the Rotary Club is to maintain community ties by creating a "sense of community." To do this, it organizes community events that bring people together, a key part of community development. Conners felt that "people need a place to interact." Califano stated that in Smithton Meadows,[3] the sense of community is growing stronger, but it is too late for her and her family. When their children were young, there were few community events. She said:

I remember it [the community where she grew up] having parades on the Fourth of July and . . . once a year they'd have some kind of a carnival or something down at the . . . little ballpark and stuff. I guess when our kids were growing up they didn't have that type of thing up here [Smithton Meadows], whereas now they do. I know they have Smithton Meadows days, and they have the winter festival, carnival whatever. But when they were little, they didn't have that. So I guess that's why . . . and now that I'm older I wouldn't go by myself. So I guess that's why I don't feel that same community like when I was a kid.

Califano also talked about the importance of a main street to the development of a sense of community. She described the town in which she grew up:

And yet, we didn't live right in the town; we were away from it. But years back you had the city type of thing, the main street with all your stores. You didn't have the malls like you have today. So I think there you had more community of feeling. Here [Smithton Meadows], I don't know why, I just don't have a real community feeling.

Wallace felt that the times had indeed changed. He stated that communities were not the same due to three factors: women in the workforce, fewer extended family systems, and increasing mobility. He said:

I think . . . there's several forces working. Number one, women, many more women, are working to support the family than before. And to a large extent, women kept neighborhoods together. The second thing is . . . by not having a community, we've become very nuclear in our own family but not outgoing to the other. And then we have a tremendously mobile society, so that people are constantly moving in and out, and you don't get to know them over extended periods of time. So there's a lot of causes here. But I would say that the concentration on the one that discourages outwardness. You're getting a little social psychology with this, but I try to look at these kinds of things.

Community Knowledge

The subjects in this research also talked about knowing the needs of others in the community, a concept critical to social engagement, as pointed out earlier. Some of the subjects felt that there was a real denial of the problems in their town. "I think this community is in a chronic state of denial. . . . We have teen suicide, but we don't have problems. We have kids on drugs, but we don't have problems" (Sharpe). A few others also mentioned a lack of awareness about social issues. "I think in Thomas Hills in particular—it's so middle class—it's easy to forget that there's a lot of people that aren't. And there's a lot of people who aren't" (Madison).

Sharpe felt that the community was well aware of what was happening in the community when it threatened the status quo or the "environment" of the community. She said:

> Well, in housing . . . he [a local developer] was going to put a huge, huge development back in there. . . . Well, the neighborhood mobilized itself [making] phone calls, watching the paper, talking about it, getting out to town board meetings, and it never happened. He did get obviously some go ahead to develop, but not on that scale. So I think this community can . . . keep its ear to the ground, so to speak, and . . . they want to maintain a kind of environment similar to what we have and will take action to do so.

James Rockford probably best summed up this idea of community consciousness:

> Well, to me, it means that you are aware of what is going on in the community; you are aware of its assets and its deficits. With that you do what you can to work to remove the deficits through participation in local government. You know, speaking to the people who have the power and the means to do something to make sure they are aware of it, as aware that you are, and that as a member of the community you feel that it is good, bad, indifferent, or whatever or get involved in it and work on it directly. I think that that's the community consciousness, that you are aware of what the community is and what it isn't. You have to have both sides of the fence.

Through their involvement in many of the voluntary associations in the community, the subjects in this research did seem to have a strong awareness of what was going on in their community. This awareness reflects Putnam's (1993) argument that people involved in civil society tend to be more aware about the community and the local government (p. 96), and with Verba, Schlozman, and Brady's (1995) argument that engagement in civil society leads to the attainment of significant political resources and a deeper personal interest in politics.

Belonging

When these people spoke about ideals of community, they also discussed the notion of belonging. Belonging reflected individual psychological needs to work for larger social purposes or toward a sense of identity. Hyland talked about an individual's need to belong: "I think people have a basic need to belong. I think it's part of our identity. We need to know that we belong, maybe to a family, maybe to a community, maybe to a . . . maybe it's just to a coffee collection, five friends that we get together with." Driscoll talked about belonging as it relates to self-respect, and when asked why belonging is important, he offered the following:

> I guess it's important because you want to feel that you're, how do I say it, contributing toward [*sic*]. I want to feel that I'm making [Thomas Hills/ Bedford Lake] a better place to live for people. And, I think I take pride, I can walk into a school, and there's no one there that's mad at me. I think there's a certain level of respect.

Smith referred to an article he had read about belonging, which he views as a social/psychological need. He said:

> I think people need a sense of being part of a social group. We say that, and then we build our little enclaves. Thankfully not in this community, but some build fences and gates. . . . There was an article in *Time* magazine last August which I heard about and read a month or so ago. The idea being that we need to feel a sense of being part of a tribe. . . . That we may look at cities like Grangeville and say that I wouldn't want to go there because of the gangs, but the gangs really have their own, they may fight, but they have their own rules, their own internal strength, which we don't have. We need to feel a sense [of belonging]; we are a social animal.

This need to be a part of something, a tribe, was also significant in Daloz et al. (1996). They also saw that it was significant to their subjects, in that a "sense of belonging and participating in a meaningful tribe is how we first begin to identify ourselves as a part of a larger social whole" (Daloz et al., 1996, p. 64). The authors continue to point out, however, that tribalism can also have a negative impact on civic identity. "Tribalism becomes particularly toxic when those we regard as different and outside are subordinated, stigmatized, and perceived as with threatening or of no account" (ibid.). They show how their subjects, rooted in their own community or "tribe," are able to go beyond that tribe and connect with others who may be different from them.

In this community-based study that lacked the diversity of many American communities, this was not discussed. What Smith did mention, however, was the article's position that suburban life actually had a negative impact on "tribal belonging." He said:

> The idea of the article [was] that suburbia is one of the worst things that have [*sic*] happened to society—psychologically. You know we have nervous break-

downs, and we have sick people who just don't have any sense of belonging. A person can drive home from work and drive into their garage, open the garage, and never talk to their next-door neighbor.

Developing a sense of belonging related to the frequency and nature of social interaction. Conners discussed some of the differences between social interaction in small towns or large cities. In small towns, he suggested that people need to rely on each other for entertainment, in contrast to large cities, where people could go to large entertainment events such as sports or plays. This reliance on community members for entertainment would suggest that small towns enhanced the social interaction necessary for a sense of belonging. However, Conners had also lived in a city and felt as if he belonged to a particular community there. He said:

> When I went to college, I lived in an area in a city, and you'd have to know your neighbors there. And, it was somewhat like a small community feeling. But then, when you went out into the broader aspects of the city, then you lost that cohesiveness. It seemed that you stuck together a little bit better.

So, in some ways, cities did and can provide localized pockets of community.

This is also true of Washington, D.C., today. Due to the political control of the city, there was a real orientation around neighborhood associations. This seemed to provide a strong sense of identity. There were neighborhood festivals and political debates. However, when most U.S. citizens are asked where they would like to live, they mention small towns (Scott, 1990).

Small towns are places where one can know one's neighbors. Conners said: "In a small town, you know the neighbor, you know what to expect from them, and that has positive and negative aspects. You know all about them, too, and that can be negative or positive. It's just the feeling that you can anticipate better, because you know . . . how they relate to others, and you meet them on the job and even socially."

Forbes points out the political practicality of that "awareness" of neighbor:

> Well, I think if you're going to live and you're going to grow, I think you've got to be able to have awareness of what the other fella's feeling, and if you don't get together and talk about it, you don't know. Somebody could have an argument and somebody says, "well, I got to have a lawyer, or I can't talk to them." This, to me, is the way it was done in a small town.

The connections between neighbors, then, also allow for the resolution of conflict to remain at a local level without institutional involvement. This reduces the cost of conflict resolution overall for both the community and the individuals involved. Indeed, many of the subjects referred to the town as lacking "issues" or "problems." When such problems occurred, individuals or small groups handled them. This ability to problem solve between and in cooperation with other community members required some stability of community members. A number of participants talked about the stability of this particular community.

Stability

The stability of community members allows for the development of a "feeling of belonging" and permits community members to know each other over time.

> There is, and again maybe this is a function of time, I have a feeling of belonging to a community of people who try and care for one another in various ways. Whether it be, you know, the ambulance, the emergency squad, or whatever. There is a feeling of belonging. Maybe that would have been true regardless of where we were if we stayed long enough. I didn't know but, of course, since we've been here forty years, that's been the bulk of our lives. So, I don't really have a basis for comparison. I can only characterize that one experience as to what my feelings are. (Witts)

Some of the reasons for the stability in this particular community reflected a history of what Rockford calls "fairly active and fairly stable farms." Bueller points out that the passing down of property from one generation to the next is also quite common. "A lot of people who have passed on homes through the generations, you know their kids and encouraged their kids to purchase property locally." In fact, many of Bueller's siblings still live in the area. Of course, as Rockford pointed out, there also has been a degree of economic stability.

Many of the people interviewed had moved here for economic reasons. This area served as a residential setting for professionals working for a large company that had its main plant in a nearby city. Today, this corporation is moving to other locations, both in and outside of the United States. In a sense, many of the people who talked about community stability lived here at a time when working for a corporation meant having a job for life.

For some subjects, moving into a new area for a job caused them to consciously work to recreate a sense of community in these new locations. Driscoll moved away from a hometown that he loved, a town where many of his friends still live today; however, when he did move here, he made it a point to "seek friends outside his family." Simmons even suggests that because many people move here, it has become a very friendly place. "On the whole, it's a very friendly town. . . . It makes it a lot easier to blend in, because everybody's trying to blend. You never feel as [though you are] an outsider."

Problem Resolution

One intended outcome of this research was to understand how the subjects resolved problems within their community, and what their perceptions were of how others resolved problems within the community. This notion of problem or conflict resolution is at the heart of politics. As Woshinsky (1995) points out, "politics is about conflict and how people deal with conflict" (pp. 21–22). He also argues that since needs are many, wants unlimited, and resources scarce, conflict is inevitable.

When asked about how problems are resolved in this community, participants' first response was often, "there aren't many problems." However, all of the subjects could think of one or two incidents, some of which were never resolved.

> We got a new post office; we couldn't resolve that. The post office has no name. It's the first no-name post office in the United States, has no zip code on it, because we cover two zip codes, and Bedford Lake wanted to be on top, and Thomas Hills has always been first. Because it couldn't be resolved, you drive down Route 25, there is a brand new post office with no name. It says United States Post Office. (Hedberg)

This incident seemed to be the exception though. Most problems were resolved, many through the actions of community members. This community action reflected a "grassroots" approach.

> I don't think we have a real . . . it's not like a city with a strong city council or government. I think if a need is perceived or problem, it is more a grassroots reaction to it. The Human Services Center is a volunteer agency. It wasn't a department created by a governmental agency. I think that when people felt that there was a lot of drinking going on by teenagers, area volunteers decided to put out a booklet of safe homes. So I think addressing problems comes more from individuals and small groups within the community than from someone above. I think it's not top down; I think it's from the ground up. I think people push to have a bike path. I think there's a lot of petitions and things like that. Luckily I don't think we have a huge number of problems. I don't think there are a lot of problems to solve. But I think that when there are it's solved more by an individual or small groups of people. (Hyland)

There was a belief in the efficacy of the individuals in the community to handle problems or issues.

> There are solutions for things. . . . Most people don't believe that anything is desperately unsolvable. They apply resources to the problem with the understanding that some problems are always going to pop up again, they will become more serious, and you'll have to try and deal with them again. That's the

way I think things function. Things tend to function through structures in place or budding off structures in place when they are not competent to handle it. (Nicols)

This belief in one's ability to make a difference in the community is particularly relevant to this study and others. Loeb (1999) discusses the significance of this to civic engagement and the modern tendency of "learned helplessness" (pp. 24–26).

The use of local mediating institutions was quite prominent. What was interesting, however, was the history of community involvement and the creation of these non-state supported civic organizations.

> The population had absolutely mushroomed in the years between 1946 and 1957. They were still years behind in the school systems. . . . But in the early days of our being here we had kindergartens, firehouses, churches, and one-room schools. Two of our children spent kindergarten in a one-room school-house in Lancaster. The community people have all kinds of advisory committees going on. We weren't involved with any of those at that time, but they helped establish curriculum and all kinds of guidelines and advisory things through the school board, so everybody was doing something. (Rockford)

One explanation offered for the high degree of community involvement was the large number of highly educated community members in this area.

> There is community support, because there are enough educated people, sometimes idle enough and have some time to put into those kind of things. When need is perceived by individuals who want to do something about it, there are structures in place to use to make it happen—the school, the Human Services Center, or their church. (Nicols)

Nicols provided another explanation for the success of the various community voluntary associations. She felt that due to the influx of people from all over the country, there were many models of community solutions available to consider.

Awareness of the needs of community members was a critical notion to the creation of these civic organizations.

> When there is a defined need, which the public sees, they respond like building their own library, like supporting the Human Services Center, their own social services organization. The library was built largely by the joint efforts of the Thomas Hills Women's Club and the Rotary Club back in the early 50s. It's been interesting this year. In times of declining school budgets, the people of this community want . . . campaigned hard to support and finance themselves from external sources a hockey team, golf, and bowling. Now adding three things like that to the curriculum at a time of opposition to taxes that

these people want programs and are willing to pay for them. And that is not exactly typical. (Michaels)

Awareness of potential or pending problems within the community also allowed for the mobilization of resources. This awareness, and the network of political resources to meet community needs, was directly connected to some of the voluntary associations in this and in adjoining communities.

I think there are too many people that just sit back and watch life go on, and they're not aware of the problems in a community. An organization, you have a chance to funnel through the organization, some situations in a community that you would know about, like with Rotary. The social worker at the school will quite often come to me and say, we have a situation, where somebody can't afford to get their furnace cleaned. And Rotary will provide the funds to clean the furnace. If we didn't have Rotary, we wouldn't have known about the situation, and many things like that come up. (Conners)

Califano describes how a fire in a local home spurred a family to call the food pantry in which she works. The food pantry then mobilized local resources. She said:

I think there's a wonderful, wonderful network, Captain of Smithton Meadows and the Human Services Center. For instance, the recent fire they had at London Square [an apartment complex in Smithton Meadows] this week. We got a call at the food pantry. They're already organizing the community as to who can help in what way. So I think it's wonderful. But again, I think you need those types of organizations to coordinate that type of thing.

Individual subjects interviewed for this research also used mediating institutions or organizational networks to resolve their own difficulties.

If I had a real problem in this community, and I wanted help in solving it, . . . I would rely on . . . a lot of people I know through church. . . . They're my closest friends, who are very connected in the town. For instance, Steve Grimes, probably one of our dearest friends, and Sam Bowler is another person, who know a lot of people, just because they're businesspeople, and so forth. And I know he could probably steer me on to who to talk to and what actions to take or who to refer to, and so forth. I'm not aware of any serious, entrenched, stubborn issues that can't be moved quickly. (Hyland)

There was also a sense that contact with a specific local public official was another productive means to resolve public issues. However, these contacts were typically informal and relied on interpersonal rather than legal or formal relations.

But if they're issues that are like town planning board or town board issues, everybody goes down to the Jenning's Market, across from the bike path, and they just have a talk with him [town supervisor]. And they chew his ear. "You should invest in a whatever it is, you should invest in another snowplow or something, or you should let the nurseries do this." (Thomas)

Thomas also described how the town supervisor helped resolve a dispute over the use of a nearby bike trail.

We . . . find that the snowmobiles are in a lot of ways a hazard. They ride up and down our road, not just behind the road, but on the road, and when there's no snow on the road, which is usually twenty-four hours after the snowfall, they ride on everybody's front lawn. . . . They seem to have no compunction about doing it. Three or four months ago . . . the president of the Lancaster Snowmobile Club came to the door to have us sign a petition to allow the snowmobilers to use the bike trail, because the snowmobilers used to use the bike trail area [before the bike trial was developed]. . . . But when the bike trail was built, it was specifically designated an area where there wasn't supposed to be any motorized vehicles. So they wanted to change that designation to allow there to be motorized vehicles like the snowmobiles. What they proposed was that they'll maintain cross-country ski trails, if there is room for a snowmobile. And I just let him have it about snowmobiles, because they ripped up lots of front lawns out here, and this is just to me very inconsiderate. And, a number of us, I know, talked to Shawn [town supervisor] about the fact that we didn't want snowmobiles on the bike trail during the winter, because we would be going cross-country skiing back there. And I find them to be dangerous when you have little kids around skiing, cause little kids are not the most sure-footed kids, and if they fall and a snowmobile is within ten feet, you just don't know what could happen. So lots of people go down and tell him, a lot of people wrote to the town board members who were charged with looking into it. And what happened was, they didn't allow the designation to change. (Thomas)

There was an understanding that people could come forward to the appropriate town board if they did have a problem, but that they had to act with a certain "style" and have some "leadership."

[When] we're after the town to do something, we just go to the town meetings and raise issues, and it takes a little style in how you do this, so you have to have some leadership. You can't go up there and be angry, even if you are angry. You got to go up there and hit them with logic they can't resist, and then you go that way. (Wallace)

Not showing anger and remaining "civil" were mentioned by a number of subjects in this study. In a meeting on sex education in the schools, Witts pointed out that, despite large numbers of people in disagreement, there was still a tone of "civility." "The high school auditorium was nearly full that night. Six or seven hundred people about evenly divided pro and con over the question . . . but, once again, they behaved rationally, civilly."

One individual even discussed how he dealt with emotional outbursts.

> Well, my technique for getting rid of the emotions is to let 'em talk, and let 'em talk themselves out. Let them get their point across, and when they're through exploding, if that's the right word, then you start to reason with them. I always try to play back what I think I've heard them say after they're through, and see if I'm interpreting what they're saying. And then I start to work on convincing them [that] this is the way to go. But you never try to fight emotions with emotions. You get no place; it's wasted effort. And sometimes it's longer. Sometimes you don't accomplish it right away. Sometimes it takes time. I'm dealing with people that I've been dealing with for years and still am not very happy with some of the things I've done, but I'm still working on them. And it's a strategy you have to learn to apply. It's fun. So I think that's the technique I follow. (Driscoll)

Developing "techniques" or "strategies" was an important part of working with others, and to be on a board meant that there were also certain norms and strategies for working with the broader public. Driscoll talked about the need for trust in these positions:

> You build trust by listening to what they want to tell you, responding to them, to accept what they are saying not to be defensive, but then always do what you say you're going to do. And once you've done it, you tell 'em you've done it. So there's that sense of closure. For the past week I've been working on a particular school issue that was making people very unhappy. That would be the staff at the Lucas Elementary School. . . . The fifth- and sixth-grade folks had a class size problem that they were unhappy with. They came to me, and I—being a public servant—did my homework and was able to convince my fellow board members that we should do something about it, and we did. We did it last night. So I called back the school this morning and said, you're going to get another teacher. Which was not in the original budget. So, I'm sure within three or four hours, it got around to all the staff and the mothers and fathers that they're going to have another teacher. It's the sense of closure that is so important.

Another interesting issue that came out of these interviews was that people who volunteered in the community often had problems with larger public institutions. These institutions did not look on these voluntary organizations and the people who worked for them as helpful in resolving problems within the larger community.

We were being very welcoming in this country to immigrants, and at the time, people from Poland were really experiencing a political demise, so we were asked to sponsor a family, and we took this request seriously. We developed a small community of people that discussed it. . . . We did a lot . . . just pulled together a lot of information and drew up a survey and went to the parish at large and asked if we could do this, would you be willing to do this. . . . The parish said yes, and so we did this. It was a very short-term program, because we said it would probably last a year to two at the most, but these are things we needed to happen. . . . So we as [a] parish, with a small core group of people, six people, decided that we could do this, and we developed the program. As part of that year, it was a real learning experience, because the volunteers had to work with the family, who could speak no English and had to begin to learn a new life. . . . We had to accompany them on all of their journeys to begin this life, and that meant going to social services. It meant trying to obtain Medicaid, food stamps, get jobs, get the kids in school, and all the things that any new family does, but this family was different, because it [the family] didn't know the language, and it was here under a lot of duress. So I remember one time having gone to Social Services to do the Medicaid application for the family, and the treatment. . . . That was my first experience with a treatment that was less than kind, and I was told in no uncertain terms about we do-gooders who have no business doing this . . . let the family take care of this on their own. I remember thinking that that was my first experience as a volunteer, with really feeling less than nothing, because the system was telling me we had no business there. And I often thought that if I weren't a volunteer and I had been representing an agency, that would not have happened. Because now that's my job . . . to go with the older person to go to the Medicaid interviews, to obtain services for them that they cannot do on their own, but as a representative of an agency and as a case worker, the doors are opened so amazingly. They are not open to volunteers. (Constantino)

Even working for an outside agency can be limiting, according to Hyland.

It's very different when you work for an outside agency in something. You have people who listen to you, some influence certainly, and there are some constraints in being separate from that. But I find now being employed by the school district I can really be more in the center of discussions and decisions.

The irony of this is clear. At a time when public support for state-funded agencies is at a low, the agencies should encourage volunteerism and work cooperatively with communities to solve problems. Instead, the social service agencies are trying to maintain their "authority" over problems and needs within the community.

A lot of the organizations are public, private, not-for-profits. You end up with issues that don't have a place with service delivery, but people become suspicious about somebody entering their area of delivery and maybe a little, well, I guess that's the whole thing today anyway. People are afraid, and everybody is competing for the same little [*sic*] dollars, which are getting less and less, so everybody is kind of protective of their territory. (Constantino)

The success of the community in the Town of Bedford to resolve problems and to support its members lies in the perception that authority is vested in the hands of the community itself. This perception requires the community to respond. While not all of the needs of community members are recognized or could be met through local means, many are. Through the work of the model citizens described in this book and the many other model citizens that work with the subjects described in this research, many community concerns are identified, the proper resources are mobilized, and situations are resolved. Instead of negating or interfering with community members working to help one another, state agencies should learn how to work with and promote volunteerism and community involvement. State agencies should help facilitate community problem solving and become an additional resource when situations require support beyond the capacity of local communities.

Involvement in Civil Society

Involvement in voluntary associations within civil society was one of the key characteristics in selecting subjects for this research. There was an expectation that subjects could be identified who valued the public good through contributions of their talents and energies. Many of the participants in this book discussed certain aspects of their community involvement that presented some patterns across interviews, including ideas of representation, types of involvement, getting started, and the "spiral of self-interest."

Representation

When the subjects in this research talked about their involvement, it was clear that they did not see their activity as political. Political activity, and holding a "political" office, was a negative role to play in public life. Politics was about balancing interests between people, rather than "advocacy."

If you're in a political office, you're always balancing one person's interest with another, or you've got to play one against the other. I'm not that type. I like that very clean, close relationship with my clientele, and this is children [*sic*] of both the community and the state. . . . I'm an advocate for children. (Driscoll)

Political activity meant that you need to raise money for your office and were therefore "politically tied" to those who gave you the money.

> A lot of money goes into the political pockets of politicians, and they in turn have got to respond to the people who donate the money. I don't want that, and I don't make decisions on politics, I make them for the kids. (Driscoll)

Being in a political position also elicited a sense that you were "self-serving," rather than community focused.

> I see different political things going on where again I guess it seems to be a self-serving type of thing. Someone will take advantage of their political position to benefit themselves rather than . . . trying to support the community and doing what's best for the community. (Adams)

Politics and political representatives were more focused on political control or power than with community problems. Michaels discussed the benefits of having politics dominated by one party and how it resolves a focus on political control. He said:

> The Republican Party has dominated the Town of Bedford, with small exception, since the Civil War. We're all Republicans. We got along. If we disagreed, it was on issues not on politics. Made for pretty smooth government. Nobody was there because they were getting rich at this job.

Of course, not all of the subjects thought that this made for smooth government. Some felt that the absence of competition in local elections led to lack of involvement on behalf of political officeholders. Hedberg said, "The Republicans have been in office for too long. They don't come to any events that the community has, like the Bedford tree lighting." She felt that this hurt the community, and said:

> The politicians didn't show up. We sent them all letters, invited them to come, and they didn't come, which is kind of typical. They don't come to anything that happens. So some of the community is lost, because you never have any of your political figures at anything.

According to Hedberg, this lack of contact leads to indecision:

> So we can't come to a decision, you can't come to an agreement on anything, and I think that has a little bit to do with the political people. They are not in touch with what's really happening in town, because they don't go to anything.

Hedberg's concerns with the distance between the local political leaders, those elected into government offices and the community, reflect what other subjects had to say about representation. Rockford believed that representatives, in an ideal situation, would be close to the people and have a genuine knowledge of the people and their lives.

This knowledge of the community and the idea of having control over community issues were significant to the participants in this research. It was felt that public problems should be resolved at a local level whenever possible and then brought up to higher levels of government when it could not be done by local means. This reflected the idea of subsidiarity[4] and the value of self-reliance, discussed earlier.

> Well, I think you can only ask the formal government at whatever level you are involved in to do so much, and then beyond that it really is the citizen's responsibility to make some sort of contribution, and there are thousands of ways you can do it. (Rockford)

One of these ways involved neighbors helping neighbors.

> There are some people who are just very, very neighborly and do things so you don't create a dependency on the local government structures to do it, because not everybody . . . even every civic organization doesn't have enough money to do the things it would like to do. (Rockford)

Rockford's views reflected the value on self-reliance, mentioned earlier:

> You should first . . . well I tend to be a do-it-yourselfer. I always tell myself I'm too cheap to go out and pay somebody to do it, but, hey, you know you should be self-reliant to as high a degree as you can. As long as it makes sense. In all aspects I think there should be a high degree of self-reliance. Whether it be on a community basis, the community should be self-reliant [sic]. When it can't do it, then it goes to the next level of the community, be it the county or the state and then, as a last resort, the federal government, but it should truly be a last resort. But there are things the federal government has to do, because it isn't realistic for anybody else to do it. But that's the general process.

Sharpe best summed up how these people felt about their role as community members, and what ideal forms of citizen representation should look like in a democracy. She said:

> Democracy is a really challenging way of life, and you can't do it by just complaining or doing nothing and not getting involved. . . . But I think it comes full circle. . . . I guess somehow I incorporated into my being the need to be involved and to be responsible for what happens around me.

Types of involvement

The subjects in this research described different types of involvement. There was involvement as "serving" on various boards, including business chambers, professional organizations, and education boards. There were different kinds of activities. Some of these people were involved with organizations that "helped people" with food, shelter, energy needs, or other economic problems. As a member of the Farm Bureau, Forbes took on the responsibility to deal with a specific issue important to the area farmers. He said: "I initiated agriculture assessment for the Town of Bedford and the Town of Lancaster, which means that those people that wanted to continue to farm had a right to be able to get [a] reduction in their taxes, providing their neighbors thought it was okay to do."

There were those who helped out in youth organizations, such as Cub Scouts, Boy Scouts, and schools and, lastly, those who focused on "community service." "The reason I became a Rotarian was because of its community service. I think that the community needs people to assist" (Conners).

Others "belonged" to organizations with which they worked, such as their church or the Human Services Center. Some were involved through their organizations in doing beyond what might normally be expected for the organization's mission. Bueller talks about one family and the aftermath of a fire at the family's home:

> What I heard—the parents ended up moving and leaving them [children]. They went to Florida, so you're talking about leaving kids sixteen and seventeen years old to take care of the house, and we ended up having a house fire there just prior to Christmas. It was proper disregard of hot ashes. The reason they were burning wood is because they didn't have any fuel oil, so once that came to light, the fire department got involved as far as with the Human Services Center. They actually donated money to go ahead and get the furniture repaired in the house. For safety reasons is the best way to put it, we [also] felt it was safer for them to heat by oil, better than wood, based on prior experience, so we helped out.

To a lesser extent, involvement was also done on an individual basis. Hyland helped whenever she was asked. "When somebody calls to bake cookies or to take tickets, I will happily do that. In terms of volunteerism, I'm not likely to find out about events, but if somebody calls and asks me, I'll probably say yes."

Sometimes Hyland could get too involved, and she reflected on the idea that there are different degrees of involvement:

> I think there are a lot of people like me, and I think there are a lot of people who take it to a higher plane, too. I don't see myself as extraordinary in this continuum. . . . There are people who don't volunteer at all, and there are people who give sacrificially of their time and money and possessions and every-

thing else. I see myself as sort of in the middle of that. I don't see myself as a saint. I try to keep it in balance for what works for us now.

Getting started

When I asked the subjects in this study how they began their involvement, they referred to three types of organizations: the workplace, the church, and schools. Of course, the subject selection procedures may have led to these organizations, but in any case, these organizations did play an important role in getting these individuals started in volunteering for the welfare of the community.

Work life and vocational development are significant to citizenship in many ways. Within a capitalistic society, one's work is entered into with an understanding that by making contributions to the community on the job, one can expect material rewards in kind. Indeed, work life is critical to democratic communities. We all need to find our place or our vocation within larger social relationships. This work is one of many of the responsibilities to citizenship. However, what these subjects revealed was that work life and public service are interrelated in numerous ways.

First of all, for some of these people, public service and community involvement led to new career patterns. Adams said that his "voluntary activities grew into a vocation." This was also true for Hyland, who said:

> While we have been in [this state], I had gotten involved in our youth group of our local church down there. And it was really a tight group. Kids would come and share a lot of stuff. I mean they would share things about their sexuality. They would share things about drinking and alcohol. There was a lot of stuff that I wanted to know more about. I mean, I could be a friend and listen, and there is some stuff I could share. But I thought, "gees, I really want, I would really like to know more about psychology and counseling" and . . . go beyond. I had a sociology major, but you know it was just an undergraduate major. So I went to graduate school.

Eventually, Hyland became an elementary school counselor.

Secondly, some forms of work seem to lead to volunteerism and/or an interest in public life. Michaels worked as a school principal for most of his life and then as a town supervisor in Bedford. He saw that "those things are occupations that have you deeply involved in the life of the community and the people. And that's the sort of natural ebb into other sorts of activities." He talked about how he got involved with the creation of the Human Services Center based on being school principal in his school's cross-town district:

> Well, for example, while I was principal of Thomas Hills High School, in the sixties and seventies, we were getting our first involvement with drug activities, a totally shocking development for a community like this. And finding

that we in the school were very poorly educated and equipped to understand what was happening, that we badly needed additional help. And out of that came the formation of the Human Services Center. We found that . . . when we looked for social services they would tell us we can't spend Towanda dollars on Thomasville residents, and vice versa. We're in a no man's land. And yet we needed programs to serve all our students, not half of them at a time. So we felt that if we establish our own local agencies that might get financial support from both counties and then administer a program we would be doing something good and useful. And I was instrumental in forming that organization. And I've been a part of [the board of] directors for so long, until a year ago, when my time on the bylaws expired.

The workplace can also provide structural incentives regarding time release or shorter workweeks. Lastly, the structure or organization of the workplace can provide opportunities for community service. Thomas was able to get involved because, for a while, he was working in less than a full-time position. He said:

> So last year, I was working four days a week so I always had Tuesdays off, and before that I was half-time for a while. And so ever since my daughter has been in kindergarten, I've volunteered in her school for a couple hours a week where her teacher knew I was coming in. For instance, on Wednesday afternoon or something, for two hours, so I would be helping out something very specific in the classroom. When I had Tuesdays off last year, I used to go in and help out, whatever time it was, 10:30, quarter of eleven, until noon, 12:15, or something like that, and I always thought that I was very fortunate to be able to do that. And it also gave me a sense of, you know, what was it like in school. What was school like for my daughter and for the rest of the kids. And having that part-time job, even if it was 80 percent like it was last year, allowed me to spend some time on the school board and still spend as much time with my kids and my family as a lot of other people.

The relations of the local business community can also provide opportunities for service. Some of these are based more on who these individuals are, and some are based on how organizations structure opportunities. Forbes helped create the local Rotary based on his friendships and connections to people he knew through his business as a local veterinarian.

The local Chamber of Commerce provided structured experiences to encourage leadership in community organizations. Mary Hedberg got involved when, for business interests, she joined the Southern Towanda County Chamber of Commerce. Individuals within that organization asked her to participate in the chamber's leadership seminar. After that experience, Hedberg was asked to serve on the board. However, she really began her involvement through her church.

The structure of church life also seemed to provide numerous opportunities for individuals in this study to get involved. While people had different motivations for this involvement, church life and structure revolved around practices of service to the greater community. Implicit in church life seems to be the obligation to service. "Well, we go to the church and I thought I should do something" (Madison). Califano recognized this obligation as part of a church identity taught to her by her parents. "And I think they did a real good job in instilling in us that your faith, and your church, has a lot to do with who you are and what you are. And . . . because of that I wanted to get involved."

The local school system also encouraged parental involvement. For many of these individuals, their involvement began by helping in the local schools. Thomas began when his daughter was in elementary school, as did Sharpe. They both went on to serve on the school board. Witts got involved when there were some financial concerns at the local high school. He said:

> I think that probably the thing that stirred me out of here the most was the fact that, when this financial crunch came in the Thomas Hills School district, I had kids in school and was concerned for what the implications or the results might be. I found out very quickly that I didn't know what I thought I knew; found out even more over the next thirteen years or so.

Witts spent the next thirteen years serving the school board as a member and as a chair.

Driscoll began with the local schools and continued to serve in larger organizations around similar issues and to spend more and more time with his volunteer work. He said:

> I got involved in community activities, having four children. . . . And then I got involved in education in 1966. I was a PTA president at Lucas Elementary School. And from there I served on a number of community committees, school committees, and then I joined the board in 1974, and been serving ever since. I'm in my twenty-second year, and been retired since 1986 and in, well, I served on the BOCES Board for eight years concurrent with my local board, so I have almost thirty years of school board experience now. And 1994, no wait a minute, no 1992, I joined the, I was elected to the . . . state school board as an area director, so at this time I serve on my local board, and also the state board. And that's almost, darn close to, a full-time activity right now, with all the legal activities and budget activities, and all the educational standards, all the work on raising the standards. It consumes most of my time, most of my daily time, and a lot of nighttime.

In all of these mediating institutions—work, church, and school—participation and community involvement were promoted. Many times these structures not only allowed for participation but encouraged it within the organization itself. Being asked to take on a position or responsibility was almost always a starting point. Many of these community organizations had some of the same members, and once you "get known," you "get asked."

> As I said, one thing leads to another, because you're involved and get known in one capacity, somebody drafts you to serve on another. For that reason, I've been involved in a large number of boards and activities over a period of time. (Michaels)

> Somebody asks you and because they've asked you, you perform, and because you perform competently or adequately, other people ask you, and it grows that way, and at some point you say there's a need, maybe I should volunteer. That's how I ended up getting involved in the chain that led me to being on the Thomas Hills school board. (Nicols)

Certainly these mediating structures are key to providing connections or networks to the rest of the community. Consider what Hyland had to say about being "disconnected" to the community and the significance of many of these community organizations:

> There are some families that . . . if their kids weren't in school, they might not really have a connection in the home. Where they're not involved in the church, they're not involved with . . . they don't really have any connections, maybe even with their neighbors. They keep to themselves.

The spiral of self-interest

Dass (1985) argues that service to others has a spiral effect on the server. The server gradually expands notions of service and her or his relations to others in the community. In much the same way, service within a community, or to any social organization, leads from self-interest to public interest. Boyte (1989) discusses this in *Commonwealth: A Return to Citizen Politics*. He points out that we must begin to engage in public life from a perspective of self-interest, rightly understood, and then move on to an appreciation of self-interest within a larger public context. For many of the subjects, their experience of service to the community began from self-interest and continued to grow into a broader notion of self-interest within the community context.

For many, this self-interest was tied up in child rearing. Parental involvement in their children's schools tended to grow in intensity, and one opportunity for involvement fed into another. This provided for a strong PTA and also seemed to develop the leadership for the school board. Witt, for example, became involved out of a concern for the financial situation of his children's school, and then he went on to serve on the school board for thirteen years.

Simmons began her involvement when a local developer started to build in back of her house. Her involvement reflects Goldrich's (1970, as cited in Nathan & Remy, 1977, p. 102) model regarding adults who were formally uninvolved in politics. Adults will get involved when they have a need, have a strategy to meet that need, and have an organization within which they can fulfill that strategy. When asked why she was involved in some of the local town boards, Simmons offered the following:

> Honestly—self-preservation. When it came down to this development behind me, I knew that they were going to have the land immediately behind me that they were going to designate as nothing more than a storm sewer. I didn't think that was a very good idea. So I went after them and said let's make park land there; let's try to keep things cleaned up. And there's about a hundred and fifty feet back there. . . . But the main reason I got involved [was] because it was my backyard and, after I got involved, I decided pretty much that the town was my backyard. And if I had any say, I might as well say it. Might as well have some authority doing it so . . . that's why I got involved.

These individuals began their involvement based on self-interest, but then self-interest grew into an understanding of self in larger contexts. Of course, self-interest was one among many motivations for participation in the voluntary associations within this community.

MOTIVATIONS TO INVOLVEMENT IN CIVIL SOCIETY

Trying to understand what motivates people based on self-report may, as Goffman (1959) might have put it, provide only a front-stage perspective without understanding back-stage realities. Whether or not we truly understand the motivations behind a specific individual's behavior is irrelevant if we can at least know what various motivations might be and, more importantly, know how to influence the socialization to particular motivations. For example, it may be appropriate to develop mediating structures that encourage a type of human development that promotes a concern for others. If, for example, an individual grows up having social relationships and social organizations that demand attention to larger social outcomes, then chances are that person may also develop a worldview that is social, a worldview that recognizes the legitimacy of self-interest within broader social contexts.

The subjects in this research discussed some of their motivations for involvement in civil society. While these motivations will be identified in this chapter, chapter 6 will describe how these motivations were shaped or

socialized over the life of these individuals. Of course, it is important to recognize that motivation and socialization are mutually reinforcing. Socialization can often set the stage for what an individual values, and values underlie
motivation. In turn, motivation leads to decisions of engagement with
agents of socialization. The primary motivations articulated by these people
had to do with identity.

The subjects in this research contextualized their behavior around their
definitions of self. Self-concepts within this research are viewed at from within
a biographical-historical approach (Cook, Fine, & House, 1995). This approach "brings in temporal considerations at the personal (as biography) and
societal (as history) levels and is concerned with the larger cultural context
within which selves are constructed" (ibid., p. 44). This study examines how
these subjects talked about themselves, and how these descriptions were used
to explain behavior.

Issue Identity

A number of subjects in this book explained their involvement in voluntary associations based on their past experiences. In a sense, they were motivated by
their identification with issues.

> My dad came from a troubled background . . . that seems to be the more you
> work with people. And I'm sure, from what you've experienced, that's just the
> way it is. There aren't really very many all-together, happy people coming
> from happy families or moving into happy families. . . . I lost my father when
> I was eighteen. . . . Then my mom just had to make it go. It was nip and tuck.
> It wasn't a very happy childhood. . . . That accounts for my interest in trying
> to work with people to help them develop themselves in ways to be more
> functional. (Sharpe)

> I had had contact with Planned Parenthood, and it does come back. I had
> had little money and a need for gynecological services, and Planned Parent-
> hood had provided them for me. Therefore, I had respect for that agency, so
> when someone came around talking about their need for board members,
> well—that is a good organization. I had personal contact with them. I know
> they have respect for women, and to me that is an important thing, so I will
> assist them. . . . I think you have to feel some connection with that need. You
> don't just do it to do it because it needs to be done. Well maybe some people
> do. But yes, I would have to say that there needs to be some sense that there
> is a personal connection to that organization and its goal. . . . I would not
> spend my time working for an agency that I have no respect for, or whose
> goals I couldn't understand. (Nicols)

Social Identity

When these subjects talked about their reasons for engaging in civic associations of various types, they almost always talked about the need for association and the relationship of that association to a sense of self. Many of them referred to themselves as "people persons." Hyland's relation to others was out of a need for "connection." She said: "I'm a real people person. . . . It's really important to connect to people, not just on superficial levels." Others talked about this same need for connection in terms of fellowship or camaraderie. "It isn't all altruism. It isn't all idealistic. It's just the joy of working with people, the fellowship" (Smith).

> I've thought about it several times, why I do get involved. Some people say I just can't say no. And, like with the Rotary, I think I like to help out within the community. I think it's important that I like the camaraderie. (Conners)

Doing as Identity

Others, like Madison and Michaels, valued themselves by their special abilities to contribute to organizations by working with others or for others. Performing service through their talents and abilities motivated them. The self was defined through action, and—by acting—the self was redefined.

> I used to be head of the aspect of the church that controls all the money for salaries. But I'm not a real money person. I mean, I like working with people, the secretaries, the pastor, that type of thing. But ultimately, I thought I really am more of a people person than a money person. So I switched jobs. (Madison)

Michaels talks about why he thinks he did "people-related" work:

> Natural inclination and a lifetime of public education, I suppose. You're dealing with all the children and all the people. School is a people business. If you compare [it] to a factory, your raw material is people, your product is people, and your tools are people. You're dealing with people and the interactions of people. All my life [referring to dealing with people], one way or another, so it's a natural association one way or another. I don't know how to do anything else.

Generational Differences

The idea of doing, of being competent, and of connecting to others has changed over the generations, according to Wallace. He said:

I think it is because of our family involvement. And I think there's been a kind
of a change in philosophy if you have the term. Most of us were born in that
same era; we were teenagers before the sixties, generally were pro what I call
"we." Not necessarily organization oriented, you know the family, community,
what have you. And then in the sixties I think there was a movement that . . .
where the "I" became much more important. And so I see a general trend
away from volunteerism. It's what I do [that] has to have immediate value to
me, rather than putting off my needs for a greater cause. You're aware also that
of course happened generally. We were brought up in a "we" era, and that has
set patterns in our lives to be associated with.

These generational differences reflect a lot of what Lasch (1978) wrote
about in *The Culture of Narcissism: American Life in an Age of Diminishing Expectations*. In modern society, our identity is socialized to focus inward and not
outward. We are, as Wallace suggests, "I" and not "we" people. This perspective
inhibits our ability to think and act within larger social structures. It inhibits
us from needing to connect to others and to see our lives caught up with the
well-being of others. But how do some of the more contemporary members of
our society still maintain a focus on the "we"?

Faith

Certainly one force for identification with others is the church. Many of the subjects explained their involvement based on their faith. To some, faith was not just
going to church but "helping other people also, and doing what I can to help humanity" (Califano). Faith was also a "journey." "I think that faith is something that
always grows; if it's going to grow, it needs to be stretched and tested, and it's more
of a journey" (Hyland). It is this stretching and testing that led to further community involvement. "You know, I believe in what my journey is, and I guess at this
point, . . . I'm deeply entrenched in my faith journey and connecting that with my
family and with service to my community and my church" (Constantino).

There also was a notion of belief in building harmony or for "caring for
others" (Smith). There was, for some, a need to "leave this world better than
when you entered it" (Driscoll). Perhaps this is not faith in a religious context,
but it suggests a belief in a much larger social arena. All of these elements of
faith require a call to action, a principal motivation, according to Coles (1993),
as discussed in chapter 3.

CONCLUSION

The key characteristics associated with the subjects in this research include a
sense of competence, self-reliance, a capacity for hard work, and a value of

social interaction over material gain. This last aspect suggests that these are people who are driven by their relations with others, and not simply by the economic marketplace.

Learning about the subjects in this book provides an understanding of why they choose to be engaged in the voluntary associations that make up this particular community. First, their identity is—in many ways—tied to the community. This community represents a place where they are known personally by numerous others. They are known through their involvement in a network of associations and organizations in the community, as well as through their interactions with others in the public spaces that are available to the community. Their welfare and the welfare of their families are tied to the success of larger public institutions such as the school system, area businesses, and the town. This community is a place where these subjects share concerns with others they know. This shared concern is the raising and welfare of children.

Because they share these concerns with others, and since they are tied to this community, the subjects in this research have become involved in numerous voluntary associations. These associations are networked and control adequate resources to promote positive change in the community. The subjects' involvement in these organizations helps them become more aware of the needs and problems of the community and believe that they can, and do, make a difference.

To resolve problems, the subjects in this research practice certain norms and qualities that promote successful conflict resolution. They believe that conflict should be rational, civil, open, and honest. As these subjects take on roles as representatives of their neighbors on the various associations and boards that govern community resources, they also take on certain ethics. They are obligated to the community members themselves, and not to personal, political, or economic ambitions. Their relationship to these community members is dependent on their ability to build trust.

Given the description of how these people think about their communities and themselves, it is now time to explore how and why they came to think and act as they do by examining the patterns of socialization that lead to these civic models of engagement in civil society.

Chapter 6

Socialization to Civil Society

This book investigates the complex socialization process that leads to a specific model of citizen. Citizens who fit this model are described as those who are actively engaged in the voluntary associations of their community and who act on the basis of enlightened self-interest (Tussman, 1997). Chapter 5 provided an in-depth description of the subjects in this study. Some of the more significant aspects of these subjects include a sense of competence, self-reliance, a capacity for hard work, and a value of social interaction over material gain. In addition, these model citizens believe that the resolution of public problems should be rational, civil, open, and honest.

Given this specific model of citizenship, the remaining question is: how do various socializing agents influence such citizenship, and are there influences that exist beyond the scope of the current literature? To investigate such a complex socialization process, it was determined that a life history method that explores real examples of citizens within a specific community would be best. The use of this method through semistructured interviews permits the exploration of current theories of political socialization while remaining open to potentially new theories of socialization to civil society.

As mentioned in chapter 4, the life history method works well in exploring individual case studies and is best presented as a life course or "career" (Bogdan & Biklen, 1992, p. 65). This notion of career is further developed in this research to refer to a specific kind of career, a civic career. The idea of a civic career suggests that an individual moves through multiple life stages in which certain developments occur that shape future experiences and developmental possibilities. Therefore, the design of this chapter reflects stages as represented by the various agents of socialization from childhood to adulthood.

The distinction between adult and childhood socialization reflects the work of Erickson and Sheehy in that these distinctions are meaningful, since the crises and conflicts presented throughout the life course vary with different age levels (Van Gennep, 1960). The type and significance of the social and mediating institutions that guide socialization are also quite different during childhood and adulthood. The mediating institutions or the agents of socialization to be discussed in this chapter include the community of orientation, family life, peers, schools, church life of any sort, and other events or activities mentioned by the subjects studied in this research and deemed significant to their civic behavior. By exploring each of these institutions, certain patterns emerged across subjects and are described in the remainder of this chapter. In the conclusion to this chapter, the significance of these patterns of socialization to civil society will be discussed.

CHILDHOOD SOCIALIZATION TO CIVIL SOCIETY

The first section of the chapter describes patterns of childhood socialization associated with the research subjects' involvement in civil society. The first significant pattern involved the types of communities in which these subjects grew up. Conceptually, this can be best described as "communities of orientation." This is based on the sociological concept of "families of orientation" (Thompson & Hickey, 1994, p. 319). Within the description of these communities and their influences on the subjects in this study, practices of reciprocity, small-town ideals, neighborhood safety, stability, and life stage similarities are discussed. The next section in the chapter focuses on family life, including support, learning certain values such as responsibility and hard work, family problems, intellectual life, developing a sense of competence, and family members as role models. Church life and its influence on leadership, social values, and social networking are then described, followed by a discussion of peers and education. Some of the themes that emerged from education include parental and teacher expectations, gender differences, activities and opportunities for involvement, the caring and attention of adults outside of the family, and college attendance. The subjects in this study also mentioned other organizations such as the Boy Scouts and the YMCA. Lastly, the influence of media related to generation and gender is discussed.

Communities of Orientation

When these subjects were asked about the communities[1] in which they grew up, they often compared their experiences to their communities today. This provided some historical comparisons that also were highlighted by the generational differences and similarities among these subjects. As mentioned in chapter 4, there was an almost even mix of subjects who came of age during World War II, or shortly afterward, and those who were in the baby boom generation. What stood out among both of these generations were the similarities in the subjects' communities of orientation.

Reciprocity

Robert Putnam (1993) suggests that reciprocity is an important social norm that strengthens social trust within a community (p. 172). He discusses general reciprocity, which "refers to a continuing relationship of exchange that is at any given time unrequited or imbalanced, but that involves mutual expectations that a benefit granted now should be repaid in the future" (ibid.). The subjects in this research were well aware of practices of general reciprocity in the communities in which they grew up. Consider a story told by Michaels from the depression era.

> I remember there was one family . . . everyone built their own house. It wasn't that you contracted for it—you built it. . . . The carpenter up the street would come down to help ya building the house. My father would go plaster his house. That sort of thing. There was a fellow doing that. His house was framed out and roofed and he died, quite suddenly. Now the widow was left with a couple of kids and an unfinished house. And my father and a couple of others went down to her and said, "we'll finish your house for you." A carpenter, a plumber, and a bricklayer, and they did finish the house to a condition she could live in. And, ironically, when my father was building a larger house, her second husband, who was a floor finisher, came up to my father and said, "let me know when your floors are ready, it won't cost you anything, we owe you for what you did before."

Some of the subjects even practiced an intergenerational form of general reciprocity. When asked why he got so involved in his community, Driscoll offered the following:

> I guess I thought that I was very lucky growing up and had a lot going for me, and I just like to feel that I can return some of that to the community. . . . I think in all the things that people did to help me, I feel I should return that to some other people.

Even though Michaels believed that this practice of reciprocity "has disappeared," some of the subjects felt that it was still strong in the Town of Bedford today. Thomas described this practice in his neighborhood today:

> There was a thunderstorm one summer night and this big willow tree came crashing down, across our driveway into the neighbor's yard and a couple of

branches hit the front porch but there was no damage to the house. . . . The neighbors from all over just came over, came over with chain saws and cut the thing out of, pulling huge pieces of the trunk out of our driveway. It was, you know, they didn't expect anything from us—they just did it. And, that's what really hit me as the fact that there are people in this community, meaning our road, who cared about us and knew that if they were in a pinch, they'd needed help, that we would help.

Another subject in this study, Conners, who grew up in the late forties and fifties, felt that although community members still help each other, more is done today through organizations.

I can remember when I first moved out here, thirty-something years ago, this fellow was up the street, was doing a driveway, and he was digging. He was going to pour cement. And I took my shovel and he said, "what do you want?" And I said, "well I just came up to help, cause I'm from a small town and that's what we used to do." If anybody needed help, we were there. You don't see that unless it's organized, nowadays.

Small towns

Another similarity among many of the subjects in this research was that they grew up or moved into what they identified as small towns very early in their lives. Conners, who had moved from a small town to a larger city, talked about what a "small-town feeling" was in comparison to city life. It seemed that in a small town, you "know what to expect" from your neighbors. Conners said:

In a small town, you know the neighbor, you know what to expect from them, and that has positive and negative aspects. You know all about them, too, and that can be negative or positive. It's just the feeling that you can anticipate better because you know them. You know how they relate to others, and you meet them on the job and even socially. When I'm talking a small town, I'm talking a thousand people. So that the interactions are much better there than in a city.

Another aspect of small-town life was entertainment and social activities. Smith talks about the small town in which he grew up:

That's like my hometown, a farming community, on Saturday night fifty years ago. The farmers came into town on Saturday night and did the shopping. They'd park their cars, their trucks on Main Street, did their shopping, and then walked up and down and visited. That was Saturday night; that was their social.

Conners contrasted the differences between large and small towns in how people practiced their social life.

In the city, you have added places that you could go, so you had a different social outlook as well. And in a small town, you had to rely on the people in the community—played canasta for hours, hearts, cards, whatever. And that was before television even. So that, when you got together, you got together for a purpose. Our [high school] senior class . . . we always went to everything together. It wasn't dating as much as it was like an amoeba. Everybody going to the same place at the same time. We used to have card parties, on a Friday night. We'd be there until two o'clock in the morning, have maybe four or five tables set up. So, yeah, that's the type of thing that a small community would do rather than, say, go to a movie, or go to a sporting event that would be available in a city or a bigger city.

Of course, today television has taken over much of our entertainment. Michaels talked about how social life has changed in his neighborhood.

We're on a street that has been very stable. We all know each other, but we don't visit back and forth. If I needed some help from any one of them and called, I would get it. That sort of thing. Every once in a while somebody plows out my driveway before I get to it, and that sort of thing. But we don't visit back and forth and have a close relationship. We don't even see them to talk to this time of year [January]. In the summer, you see people. We are more insulated from each other. With television and what have you, we're less dependent upon our neighbors for companionship. Different times . . .

Neighborhood safety

Another aspect of these communities of orientation was that they allowed for a degree of insulation and "protection" from the outside world. There was a sense of safety and security in the community.

The kids I hung around with were all the same. . . . We were prior to the drug and alcohol and cigarette scene. Nobody did that, and only one girl in our class became pregnant. I remember at that time and it was just you know the shock of it all. . . . It was a very small town, and we were so protected we had no idea about the bigger picture. (Constantino)

This idea of safety was prevalent among many of the subjects. Although not all neighborhoods had the type of homogeneity to which Constantino referred, many of the World War II generation subjects grew up in ethnically diverse neighborhoods, but these neighborhoods were also very "safe."

I think you're always safe in your own neighborhood. God, if you did anything wrong there was always some mother that saw you. And you know they [the mothers] were kinda the watchdogs of the neighborhood. (Wallace)

However, this neighborhood structure of support and safety was not specific to living in small towns. Thomas who grew up in a dense metropolitan neighborhood, also talked about his neighbors and their interdependency:

> When I lived in Macklin [an urban area], we lived in row houses. Actually, not row houses, they were all basically cookie cutter, they were the same houses; there was about fifteen feet between each house, just enough for a driveway. There was a tiny driveway and a tiny garage. My father never even had a garage, and our neighborhood was, for the most part, our block. You know, because there were a lot of people living in a relatively small area. But the thing that was neat about it was that you were very close to [your] neighbors. The people that lived next door to us, which was about, like I said, fifteen feet away, they were like an aunt and an uncle to us. They were older than my father, fifteen or twenty years older than my parents. But . . . if she [his mother] had to run to the store, she'd call over to Aunt Bess and say, I've got to run over to the store, could you come over and watch the kids for a few minutes? They were not related to us, but they were Uncle Peter and Aunt Bess. . . . We'd walk across the street, and we were seven or eight years old. And we'd just tell our mother we're just going over to the Barkers' and so we'd go over to the Barkers' house across the street and play over there all afternoon. So it was a really nice place to grow up at the time when we, when I was young. I'm trying to think what grade we were, I must have been fifth or sixth grade when we moved to another house four blocks away—a bigger house 'cause there were then six of us. And that was also still a pretty closely knit community. You know, you can walk down the street, and call for a friend, and I was ten years old, eleven years old, no big deal. I'd get on my bike and go across town and just hang out with my friends. . . . As long as I told her where I was going, I was done. What time do I have to be home? Be home at five or five-thirty or whatever. And it seemed like . . . they never gave it a thought.

These close relationships between neighbors and the identity of neighborhoods also crossed generational lines. Compare Thomas's quotation, and his neighborhood of the 1960s, to Witt's view of his 1930s' neighborhood:

> The street we lived on was fairly stable in the sense that people didn't come and go. They lived there for extended periods of time. We lived there from 1932 until 1945. I had left for college before my parents moved from that street. As a consequence, there was a certain stability in relationships. There was a neighborliness involved. When my grandmother, who was living with us at the time, became ill with pneumonia and subsequently died, the next door—I was only nine at the time—the next-door neighbor took me in and kept me for that whole period, fed me, and I slept there in the house and that sort of thing. We were back and forth across the alley, the double driveway all the time.

Stability

One of the keys to this "neighborliness" might be the stability of which Witt spoke. Families moved into these neighborhoods when they were beginning to have children and generally stayed there for the rest of their lives. The subjects in this research, across generational lines and demographic settings, all spoke of the stability of their neighborhoods, and this neighborhood stability was also true in the Town of Bedford today. Bueller describes the stability of his family and those around him:

> There's a lot of us [his family] who still reside in Bedford Lake: my brother Bob, my brother Tom, my brother Joe, my sister Pam, she still lives in Bedford Lake, my sister Lisa she lives right over here in Smithton Meadows, just outside of Bedford Lake, and I have another sister that lives in Bedford Spa. Out of all of us, only one sister really lives outside of the area, and that's my sister Sheri, who lives in Rhode Island. I guess that's the point I'm trying to say to you—you see a lot of family, still stay within the community itself and not venture outside.

Of course, the stability found in the subjects' communities of orientation was generally relative to a single generation. Most of the subjects in this research grew up in communities in which there were no multigenerational ties. Their parents had moved into the area and had raised their families. Often the next generation, in this case, the subjects of this study, moved to other communities to raise their children.

Baumgartner (1988), in a study on suburban life, suggests that this limitation on stability helps reduce the possibilities for confrontation, due to the following:

> A culture of weak ties seems to undermine confrontation and promote moral minimalism in several ways: (1) it renders forceful action against antagonists less compelling by holding out the likelihood that a subsequent departure of either party will take care of the problem in the normal course of events, while it meanwhile makes avoidance a feasible option; (2) such a social order also makes bitter enmities and resentments difficult to sustain and limits the ability of people to accumulate damaging information about one another, partly by keeping offenses relatively private and out of the public view; (3) a system of weak ties lessens involvement in any single relationship and leaves people little time to manage conflicts within it; and (4) it deprives people of cohesive bands of allies or other supporters to assist them in pressing grievances, whether through violence or negotiation. In practice, these implications generally coexist and appear to be cumulative in their effects. (Baumgartner, 1988, p. 92)

This reflects the comments made by Simmons, who felt that by moving into a new community, she did not have to face the tensions that develop over generations in a more traditional community. This may help explain some of the "neighborliness" that these subjects felt. They had no histories with one another, and they could avoid each other if problems did arise (Baumgartner, 1988, pp. 73–74).

The other side of this is that genuine community is not realized. Problems may be ignored to avoid confrontation. It is the politics of "voting with your feet," a concept of the Reagan administration, whereby if you do not like the local circumstances, economic or otherwise, you simply move on to a new community. This moving and avoidance of civic dilemmas do not necessarily promote the skills and perspectives needed to participate in civil society. There is no need to learn how to deal with conflict or to understand the importance of dialogue and debate. The building of social capital can also be stunted and can gradually impact the larger questions of public life within that community. This type of community, as Baumgartner (1988, p. 92) suggests, is a result of weak ties and fails to hold the potential for Barber's ideal of a "strong democracy" (Barber, 1984). So, on the one hand, old traditional animosities are erased, but on the other hand, the potential for a "failed community" can be that much higher, particularly if there is a lack of stability. Fortunately, in this community there was generational stability as well as life course similarities that brought people together.

In terms of explaining why there was such stability in the Town of Bedford, Rockford suggested that it was due to the agricultural nature of the area. However, since Bueller and others who were not in agriculture also mentioned the stability of the community, the better explanation might be economic. Earlier in the history of the community, agriculture provided economic opportunity, as suggested by Rockford: "It's a community that has been fairly stable in that it has been historically composed of fairly active and fairly stable farms." Later on, economic growth in manufacturing provided a steady source of jobs as more companies moved into or developed plants in nearby Thomasville.

Life course similarities

Partially due to the economic development of the area, many families moved into the Town of Bedford at similar stages in their life course, when they were beginning to raise families.

> When we moved into the house—the next two houses down—we all moved in within six months of each other, and we formed a close alliance over the years. We're kinda like family, even though you know we came from all different spectrums. (Wallace)

Some of our subjects not from this area also discussed how their communities of orientation were filled with families during the same stages of child raising.

Our neighborhood . . . started building around the same time, the late fifties. Everybody who moved in were probably, oh, adults in their early 30s who had one or two children and had one or two more while they were there. So there was a pack of kids all at the same time. (Simmons)

People coming together in communities during similar events or life stages also occurred for the older subjects, who grew up in the 30s and 40s. For these subjects, a common bond developed from a similar pattern of immigration. "Ethnic" neighborhoods worked together to deal with the stresses of family life in a new and growing country. Often, unrelated families had to depend on each other almost as extended kin in more traditional communities.

The subjects' comments about these neighborhoods and their interdependencies are reminiscent of Stack's (1975) book *All Our Kin: Strategies for Survival in a Black Community*. In both cases, kinship was not by blood but built on the interdependency of economic and child-rearing needs. Bellah et al. (1992) also point out the benefits of developing these interdependencies. They suggest that "commitment to a community turns out to be a much stronger basis for an effective economy than the individualistic pursuit of self-interest" (p. 94).

Conclusions

The communities of orientation for these subjects seemed to promote communal engagement in the shared practices of child rearing and social life. These practices led individuals to see their own and their families' well-being tied to the community. The community was a source of entertainment and support in the daily tasks of child care. They also felt that their neighborhoods were safe for their children. Neighbors looked out for each other's children, and a mutual reliance on one's neighbor in times of stress could be expected.

Underlying these safe, stable, family-oriented communities were specific economic trends tied to migration and job security. Without steady jobs, the stability of the community and its members becomes threatened. This stability allows for the development of networks of mutual support and assistance. However, especially among those of the World War II generation, there was a feeling that community life in Bedford and across the country was indeed changing.

There's several forces working. Number one, women, many more women are working to support the family than before. And to a large extent women kept neighborhoods together. The second thing is we're . . . by not having a community, we've become very nuclear in our own family but not outgoing to the other, and then we have a tremendously mobile society so that people are constantly moving in and out, and you don't get to know them over extended periods of time. So there's a lot of causes here. (Wallace)

A few subjects suggested that a relatively mobile society is not necessarily detrimental to community life. Driscoll, from the World War II generation, talked about moving from his hometown to the Town of Bedford, and how he took the initiative to meet new people and establish new friendships. "I got married in 1949 and joined Montauk Electric, moved away from my hometown. And we've never moved back there, so we've always had to seek friends outside of our family. It's a good life."

Certainly changes in community life are important to consider. Many of the subjects in this research, whether they grew up in small towns or large cities, described how well they knew their neighbors through common social practices. These social practices are significant to the development of social networks that lead to recruitment and to a sense of a shared public life (Putnam, 1993). Whether people know each other through bowling leagues or by exchanging hellos on a main street on Saturday night, this familiarity provides a key element of what community means according to the subjects in this research. Community to them meant being known and knowing others (see chapter 5). Furthermore, belonging to a community meant that there was an attachment of self-identity to the community, or an understanding that self-interest is tied to a larger social context. Belonging to a community encouraged individual awareness and an enlightened self-interest.

Family of Orientation

Family life and other mediating institutions that connect to family life, especially school and church, probably had the greatest influence in terms of value development. It was also the family, particularly the parents and grandparents, who also modeled participation in community life or, in other ways, created the values and motivations that led these subjects to become involved later in life.

Family support

Most of the subjects in this research came from very supportive family structures in which "family always came first." Being together, especially on holidays, was valued, and children received a lot of attention.

> My kids got teased . . . Chris used to come home and say everyone refers to us as the Ozzie and Harriet family. Well, that's—in a way—how I grew up. No family is ever perfect. I'm not trying to put on that kind thing, but . . . if you lived in the country, family always came first and church and activities. We always did things together, celebrate holidays together, got involved . . . we did connect with other families, with other people. But often our family

would be doing something and we would invite others to come along with us type of thing. (Hyland)

Families were often referred to as "close knit" or "tight."

I come from a large family. I have three brothers and four sisters. . . . When I was growing up, the family . . . everybody got along real good. It was nice growing up with a big family. I'll tell you for a large family, we did do a lot together. Pretty tight, I guess you would call it. (Bueller)

There was also a lot of "support" and attention. Four of these subjects were only children or had siblings who were fourteen years or more older and received a good deal of attention from adults in the family. Constantino, who had to leave her parents at a young age, was able to find support from her aunt and uncle. She said:

You know, I think if it hadn't been for my uncle, I'm not sure what I would have done because he had stopped drinking the first year we went there, and he's the one who really nurtured me and prepared me to go on. He was a very sensitive, intuitive person, so he wanted the best for both my brother and myself. He helped us to get that and helped send me to school.

This practice of attention often was reflected in the discipline of children. There was a clear sense of "right and wrong," and subjects often referred to a "strict" upbringing.

I think basically as you were maturing if you did something wrong he [his father] would basically explain to you why it was wrong, and if you didn't respond by his explanation, he would resort to other means if necessary. No, I don't mean he wasn't no [sic] abuser at all, but he was strict. He was a disciplinarian, and he expected you to respect himself and my mother. . . . No, he was good. I wouldn't say he was over strict, but basically how he explained things so you knew the difference between right or wrong. (Bueller)

Califano learned to be independent because of this strictness. She said:

They were strict, no question about it. When they had proms back then, they used to have what they call, they have the afterglow parties, they had after-prom parties. And my parents would not allow me to go. They didn't feel it was appropriate for a girl to be out all night. . . . But I think because my parents were that way, I think that made me a stronger person. . . . In what way? I don't know, because I was different. I wasn't allowed to do a lot of the things that everybody else would do. You weren't allowed to go along with the crowd. And I think that makes you stronger; it makes you a stronger character.

In Daloz et al. (1996), this notion of not being able to go along with the crowd or of having values that may not fit within the majority is referred to as "value-based marginality" (p. 74). The authors found that one-third of their sample experienced this, and that it helped "foster the capacity to care for the common good" (ibid.). This also relates to the influence of religious life, in that religion can teach values and morals that are not necessarily in step with more mainstream values. This will be discussed later in this chapter.

Sometimes the "strictness" or high expectations were the motivations for involvement later in life.

> That was difficult because, as I said, my father was the principal of the school. And the threat was always if you got it once at school, you got it twice at home. And I was brought up that you represent the family and you reflect on me as well as on you, and that was my father speaking, and that was difficult, and that was a difficult thing to live up to. And I think that is part of the situation I have now, is mainly why I get involved as much as I do. Because I'm always looking for recognition. (Conners)

Learning values and virtues

The values and virtues most held by the subjects in this research, mentioned in the previous chapter, were heavily influenced by family life. The best example of this is the sense of responsibility gained from being an important contributor to the family. These subjects had specific tasks to be completed that helped the family survive. Later on, in their adult lives, this same sense of responsibility was present in their work in voluntary associations.

Their family responsibilities began at an early age. Many of the baby boomer families had two incomes or came from large families that required everybody to work. When Califano came home from school, she did "all the cooking and the cleaning" for her mother. As the oldest daughter, Nicols was the one "left responsible" when her parents were out. She said:

> So, I'm the older of two daughters. I think that kind of responsibility does affect the choices you make in later life. "I'm going to the store, while I'm gone I want you to dust the furniture in the living room and do the dishes." Therefore, I was left responsible to see that the work gets done by the younger brother and sister. Mother goes off to have her back operated on, spends months in the hospital when I'm seventeen years old. I'm left to organize the household.

Thomas's mother intentionally taught her children to be responsible after she realized that she did not teach this to her first two children.

> After those two boys having gotten to a certain age, my mother realized that she had done it all wrong, and that the rest of us were going to learn how to

pitch in and do everything around the house, and we did, we learned everything. I mean, I'm convinced that to this day that the reason I know how to do everything around the house, cook, clean, the only thing I can't do is sew, bake, all that stuff—is because my mother basically said to herself, "these kids, and I, am [sic] going to be much better off if they're all doing this stuff, and I'm not doing it all." And so that's the way it was. (Thomas)

Both Driscoll and Forbes grew up on farms. Driscoll's father was injured while Forbes's father died when he was young. Both had to do all of the work. Driscoll described his life on his family's dairy farm:

And so when I was born into the world, I was born into a dairy farm where, when I was nine years old, my father was injured by a bull very badly. And from that day on, I had to work on the farm as long as I lived there, until I went into the service. So my life was always work, and school, and fun. It was a good life, because twice a day I had to milk the cows, before I went to school in the morning, so my day started generally at five o'clock in the morning, and then I'd come home from school, milk the cows again. So it was a very laboring life, but then I had a lot of fun.

To Forbes, the responsibilities of farm life were distinct. "There is a difference, and so if you're a farm person, the animals get fed before you eat. You go out there [at] five in the morning, and they get fed, they're milked and they're fed. You go back out after you've eaten and kicked the feed back in. It's all sort of a ritual, but you know where your work is." Both Driscoll and Forbes were an important part of the organization that was the family.

All of these subjects had to take on responsibilities not only for themselves but also to ensure the well-being of their families. Family as a model for future involvement in "organizations" might provide a partial explanation for these subjects having such a sense of responsibility to their communities and valuing the self-reliance of their particular neighborhoods or communities.

Nicols had a similar situation and felt that "it's somewhat a question of learning that you have responsibilities in the organization you live in. The organization I lived in was my family, so I learned to have responsibilities."

Troubled family life

Motivation for involvement in the many voluntary associations of civil society also came from situations in which family life was anything but supportive. Some tragedies of family life (alcoholism, loss of contact, or lack of emotive support) created a need for some of the subjects in this research to reach out or to do better. This finding was also found in the Daloz et al. (1996) study: "In about one-third of the families, a parent had died, was absent, disabled, or otherwise dysfunctional" (p. 28).

This study and Berkowitz's (1987) study emphasize the influence of parenting and the overall role of the family. Earlier studies in socialization also support the view that the role of the family is critical in determining how children view the world and how they understand their roles in the world (Davies, 1977). Sears, Maccoby, and Levin (1957, in Davies, 1977, p. 165) found that parents' acceptance or rejection of their children had an impact on their children's abilities to develop an internalized sense of morality. These subjects, who faced adversity in their families, not only overcame this adversity, but the troubles in their families of orientation also motivated them to achieve in public life.

Hedberg came from a family that was not at all supportive, yet she overcame that and has become quite active in the community. The quote that follows is contained in her brief biography in appendix D.

> They didn't want me. Mother was very religious, so she wouldn't get an abortion. . . . I had three siblings. I have a sister, and I have two brothers, or I had two brothers. My oldest brother, they didn't want because he was born too soon after they got married, so it looked like they had kids before they got married, which was really stupid, God, fheuf! Now everybody is going out and doing that. So they didn't want him. My sister, they had to wait, she didn't come right away. So they had to pray for her. So she is beautiful, she's intelligent. She is wonderful. She is marvelous. She is elegant. She's Cathy. You can't say enough wonderful about my sister. Then my younger brother was born with Rh negative blood. They took him to the hospital. They had to pray so that he would be better, so my parents just idolized him. Once again, they paid for him to go to college. They paid for my sister to [go to] college. David and I were, were too stupid. We were too ugly. We were too worthless to pay to go to college. They took the family and two of them they liked and two of them they hated. And when my younger brother died, I met my parents at the airport, and they said they wished and prayed to God it had been me—that I had a worthless life, and he had lots of value. Then it was like okay, good, I'm glad I met you at the airport. To my mind, it has become a game with them, to see how angry they can get. . . . It is very upsetting to them for me to have gotten to where I'm at.

Hedberg also said that it "was the way my parents treated me, influenced me, as far as I worked a lot harder." Later in life, this hard work and her involvement in the community helped her see that she did have "qualifications." She added:

> So that's what I grew up with. This negative attitude. My parents still call and say "Oh, we wish you had never lived." I said "Thank you, I'm so glad you

called." Why do you care? I felt I had to go out and I had to make people like me. But then I found out that I didn't really have to make people like me, because I also had qualifications. I had value as a person. So organizations helped me realize, that as a person, I had qualifications and values, which was a big surprise.

Hedberg was not alone with her family life struggles. A few subjects discussed alcoholism as a factor in their family life. Again, however, the negative was turned around into a motivating factor.

My family had severe alcoholic problems, so there was a lot of that ACOA [Adult Children of Alcoholics] stuff. . . . So a lot of that dysfunction remains with me, because I have trouble separating from other people because of that, because I need that connection. It's really important, but I think because of that . . . I'm a very sensitive person and very aware of where I fit in to the bigger picture, and I have very deep faith, very deep. (Constantino)

Sharpe also came from what she called a "dysfunctional" family. Her father did not like his job and was always trying to get ahead and be his "own boss." Consequently, he did not always have time for family and could get "moody." She said:

Once in a while my mother and I would play, and on very rare occasions my father would play with us, and that was a real treat. . . . My recollection is he would work nights. He'd come home in the wee hours in the morning and go downstairs to his office and work there. I just remember going down and saying good morning and then that was it. When he was around he was very moody and very volatile, so in our house you just watched dad's face and knew whether you better watch out. . . . The one thing I always remember is playing with him in the waves at the beach. You're probably going to see some tears with this one, because there's a real void in my life in terms of bonding with dad.

Sharpe's father died when she was eighteen.

Thomas also had to deal with loss when his older brother ran away from home. He said:

We moved into a corner house—we lived in two different houses when we lived in Macklin. The corner house where we lived had three floors; it had five bedrooms, so my oldest brother had his own room, but Paul, who is the one that is three years older than me, who I was pretty close with, he and I continued to share a room. And he ran away from home when he was seventeen, I guess. Which in our family, an old Italian family, nobody did it. He had problems with my parents because he dated a lot. He was always out late, and so my parents were pretty strict about him being in at certain times. And Paul was just a real rebel and couldn't understand why. And so he left home and came back . . . in a few weeks or about a month later, and was home for a few months and then left again and never came back. He ended up getting married when he was nineteen and divorced, I think, by the time he was twenty-five or twenty-six. But when he ran away and got married, nobody from my family went to his wedding. . . . It hurt me when he left home, because he was like one of my best friends. And, he was just gone. And you know I was relatively young, so I had no contact with him when he left.

These subjects all faced either a sense of loss or detachment to their parents or to others in their immediate family. For some, this loss or detachment led to a need to be connected to others, to be in a relationship with others, constantly trying to recoup that loss. For Hedberg, her parents' disregard of her person led to a need to prove that she was worthy. Her involvement helped her to realize that and to make a difference in her thinking about herself. All of the subjects who faced adverse family situations were able to find personal growth and fulfillment through their involvement in the voluntary associations of civil society.

Intellectual life

Family life, and parents in particular, promoted the intellectual life and the value of education held by the subjects in this book.

My father was a bricklayer who had no education beyond the eighth grade. Had to go to work to help [the family] . . . he was the oldest child in his family. His father was an abusive alcoholic. He had to go to work to help his mother, Irish Catholic family. For a person who had lifelong interests in intellectual things [*sic*]. Reading, he was an avid reader all his life; [he] always was very interested in history, American history. And as I grew up, I said here was a fine mind who could have profited a great deal from education, but he never had an opportunity. My mother went to Easton High School and dropped out at the end of the third year because of health reasons, although she lived until she was ninety-eight. Grew up in a very supportive home, which supported education. Two parents, neither one were a high school graduate, yet were determined that their children were going to get a college education. They made a great sacrifice to help me as much as they could. (Michaels)

Michaels also talked about how he debated with his father around the dinner table and used these discussions in his classes:

He always wanted to talk politics and that sort of thing. Discussions around the table at home, and I used to like to argue with my father so . . . I would take a management versus labor viewpoint. He didn't know that, in sociology classes, I was using what I was learning from him in a counterdiscussion.

Another subject, Nicols, also had a family who lacked formal education but valued learning:

> My father is an avid reader, learner, and thinker about things. Formal education I think finished in the sixth grade. He always took two newspapers, morning and evening. He had opinions about things, so he's [a] model, in a way, of the fact that because you are not educated does not mean you cannot be intelligent or be involved in your community.

Siblings also played a part in the intellectual life of the family. Nicols came from a "family of talkers" who argued and debated at the dinner table. Political discussions were also part of life for a few of the other subjects in this book.

The implications of the form and practice of these debates relate directly to the subjects' current practices in the public life of their community today. Many of the subjects in this research felt that public problems should be resolved through open, honest, and rational debate. This view of resolving public problems might be learned through formal education, but it might also be the result of reasoned debate, by parents and siblings, at the dinner table.

Another interesting aspect of intellectual life among these subjects was familial interest in music. Five of these subjects talked about music and family life, or how their parents played or participated in some form of musical group. While it is unclear how this relates to voluntary behavior in civil society, Daloz et al. (1996) suggest that it can create a "central source of connection and renewal" (p. 86). Certainly the role of music and its value to intellectual life and social behavior is worth further study.

Role models

Parents were role models in a variety of ways, including the promotion of values and virtues. However, there were direct examples of parents modeling voluntary behavior in their communities. Califano, for example, saw her parents as being very "giving people," and she recalled this Thanksgiving story as an example of their actions:

> I can remember one Thanksgiving my father knew of a family. Maybe this had something to do with who I am, what I am, today. But he knew of a family because, again, he used to travel around to all those remote counties and stuff. There was a family that was having difficulty. And I can remember one Thanksgiving we cooked a turkey and brought a turkey to them. I don't know who they were, but I can remember bringing this turkey to 'em.

Simmons refers to her mother and grandmother to explain how she decided to let her "views known" when speaking in public forums. She said:

> Both my grandmother and mother have always been the same kind of people, . . . able to stand up and say what they believe at town meetings and things like that. [This was] back in the twenties and fifties where the majority of women at that time were "stay at home and let my husband do all the thinking." Neither of the moms in my family were ever like that. As I said, though, I was kind of a mouse when I was a little kid. When I got to be an adult, I decided it was time to let my views be known. Must be something to do with them.

Nicols sees her involvement not as an obligation but as something "you just do." She believes that she learned this from her parents, particularly from her mother:

> My father was a city councilman; both my parents were presidents of the benevolent association they belonged to. My mother is a doer, a helper. I think you learn without even thinking, you're learning by observing what goes on in your family. I would expect at some point my children are likely to become involved in organizations and to be able to do things in their community. Not necessarily even because they thought they ought to. I never thought I should, this is my responsibility. I just thought I want to. Some of that must be from observation, because that's what *grown-ups do*. They become involved, and I don't think they can teach that in school. They have to see it.

Parents also could be negative role models when contrasted with other adults who may have been from a former generation, as was the case for Madison. She explains how she learned or developed from her grandmother a need to "give back":

> You learn it sometimes through church. There's a particular pastor who speaks to that a lot. I like to hear that. I think people need to hear that. . . . I was conscious of when I grew up of my parents not giving back, and my grandmother giving back. I was real close to my grandmother, who did a lot of things for people. I mean she did it constantly. And yet her son was a different kind of person, real cerebral, a lawyer. . . . He does now, but he didn't as a child. When I was a child and my mother, for whatever reason, is not a people person. So she didn't. But I liked being with my grandmother; I liked visiting the sick people I went to see with her. . . . I thought she did the right thing. I wanted my parents to do more when I was younger, but I didn't let them know that. I just thought they should. So I chose to live differently.

Sharpe talked about how she learned to become a leader. Leadership to her meant those "who are willing to get out in front, get information out, and encourage people to take action." She felt that, to some degree, she had learned these things from her mother. She explains how leadership is learned:

> What they experience growing up I think is a major factor. In my case, my mother was involved. Now she is active in the church in terms of music. She was active, I think she taught church school. I can't remember. She was active in the Y, again with music. I mean, she was just a doer. So what they experi-ence in childhood, their innate abilities I guess in part [sic]. I think the phi-losophy besides the parents being a role model in terms of doing but also in terms of being. You know, what is life about, what are our responsibilities, you know, that whole aspect of that.

Siblings also set a direction to be followed. Driscoll followed the example of his brothers in joining the Army Air Corp during World War II, and Bueller followed his brothers in joining the local fire department.

While peers often become more influential in the socialization of chil-dren as they grow older, the families of these subjects provided examples of the type of citizenship being explored in this book. It is likely that these ex-amples were reinforced later, either by childhood peers or peers in adult life. In any case, having role models to set examples is essential to the formation of citizenship. It is a fundamental necessity for children to have examples of behavior to follow, and it is clear that for the subjects in this research, they were available.

Church Life

Verba, Scholzman, and Brady (1995) found that religious institutions are often the places in which individuals develop civic skills. In this research, we found this to be true, but the influences mentioned had more to do with value struc-tures and with the development of how these individuals defined themselves and their role in the world. As mentioned earlier, this was significant to the "formation of commitment" found in the subjects in Daloz et al.'s (1996, p. 141) study, and it also reflects the research done in Bellah et al.'s (1985) *Habits of the Heart.*

> For all of them [referring to three subjects who are involved in churches or synagogue], religion provides a conception, even if rudimentary, of how one should live. They all share the idea that one's obligations to God involve one's life at work as well as in the family, what one does as a citizen as well as how one treats one's friends. (Bellah, 1985, p. 239)

The relationship of church to family life also seemed more direct than some other mediating institutions.

I guess that my faith has always been, my faith in God has always been key and central in life from the time I was really tiny, and it was central in growing up in my nuclear family with my mom and dad and my brothers and sisters. I think that particularly my mom was . . . but it was key to my father. It was just my father, and I think to some degree, it's always been a connection I've had with my dad. (Hyland)

Some of these subjects saw the church as the moral balance of their parents' views.

I think that through the church I carry . . . you can claim yourself, you can get satisfaction from . . . you can give, get, or receive a value system that doesn't necessarily have to relate to your value system as a child. If you're paying attention, you can grow. I don't think I'll ever be Christ-like, but I think I have gotten a lot of direction through my faith as to how I should react to different things and how I can't dislike my parents because of their negative attitude toward me. (Hedberg)

For Wallace and Thomas, the church and its teachings provided a balance to social views on war.

I guess I do look at religion specifically and . . . Christ's teachings—I view myself as really much more of a peacemaker when it comes to my political beliefs. I'm looking at how politics and government impact the lives of all of us as well as the world. Four years ago, it's five years ago now, when the Gulf War was going on, we were protesting in front of the Towanda Post Office. . . . Every day we would vigil before that war started. . . . That was almost the first time I really kind of demonstrated and made my beliefs about something very public. And . . . it was just so obvious to me what we should be doing and what we shouldn't be doing in terms of that war. (Thomas)

Wallace began to reflect on the teachings of his church when confronted with the reality of the social norms during World War II.

All of those people were conditioned by the Second World War and the psychology of the Second World War. And we ended up hating Germans and Japanese. And you got to be taught to hate. And it's very relevant, because you're much more effective if you're going to fight to have that latent in your background. Even if you're in your church and it says love thy neighbor, but they weren't neighbors. It was interesting because I was down at the solar energy conference in 1961, and we got up early to take some pictures of cherry blossom time. And there was another person down at the bottom waiting for the elevator. And he was Japanese, as it turns out. We started talking, and he was a med [medical] student down at Duke, married, a couple of kids. You know, same general background, and we started talking and you start to realize that that person happened to be in the Japanese Marine Corp. You start interacting with him on an eyeball-to-eyeball level. And this is a stupid thing of hate. I think the church teaches you that, but you get caught up in the time, where there becomes certain other priorities. (Wallace)

Church also "did things for you" or taught you "lessons." Nicols learned "what was acceptable." She said:

You learn at home, and you learn through church that society has different expectations of you with behavior, and that there are things outside yourself that are important. In that instance it is doing the right thing so you don't go to hell, also the glory of God; pick, make a choice. So definitely being actively involved with the Catholic church and Catholic education did have an effect—my perceptions of what was acceptable.

Simmons saw the role of the church as being critical to learning one's position in the context of a community. She said:

I definitely think that there should be more interactions between community and church life. As far as just being able to, as they're [children] growing up, as they're forming opinions, be able to make that mix, so I see how that works in this situation. And so when they want to decide what they want to do, they have a good, solid base to make their decisions on. And growing up the way I did, with both Catholic and Protestant views on things, it left me with a much broader attitude. Although I can't personally stand the structure of having to go to church, I think I have a very strong religious attitude. I just don't like the structure of being told exactly what I should believe. So I stay away from that part. And if my kids choose to do that, then fine. They're basing it on some knowledge, not just on feelings.

Conner's experience in religious education classes taught him to "feel good associating with others." He said:

I think it was more or less the fact that you went to church, you went to meetings. When you first went, you were there to be, maybe to listen to others. But after a while, you became the ones they were listening to. I can remember in high school, I used to teach Sunday school to the younger kids. And it was because I had been brought up in the church and I knew the stories, etc., and I became the one that was telling them the stories and boring them to tears, just like I was a few years before. I tried to be more active, because I can remember going through it. But, no, I felt that I became very involved because of what it did for me. It made me feel good. It made me feel good that I was associating with others.

One of the subjects in Daloz et al.'s (1996) study even found that "unlike the school, church proved to be a place 'where most of the time I felt more equal and could play a lot of leadership roles'" (p. 127).

Wallace learned about an "extended family of human beings." He explained how special discussions in church influenced his thinking:

> I think the first way—early memories—is Dr. Brown talking about the needs of the Eskimos. He was a great friend of Sir Winford Grenville, who did a lot of things up in Greenland. And you start becoming aware of an extended family of human beings that have needs, and you start being concerned about it. It takes you beyond the community.

Church also taught about purpose. It promoted an active life of service to others through the church and through vocation. Hyland is an example of how the church's teachings influence not only involvement in the community but on the job as well. She said:

> I think if I weren't involved in church, it's not like my parents, my mother who's still living, would scorn me or anything. It's just part of who I am, so I do that. I enjoy music tremendously, and that's part of a draw for me, but I also enjoy connecting with people. And I find that believing in a purpose beyond myself is real important. Rather than just the day-to-day, hand-to-mouth kind of living that, or just accumulating things. It's really important to me to be connected to people, to feel good or worthwhile about what I do. Which is probably the reason I'm a counselor.

Thomas also saw how the church led him to a career in which he needed to have a direct impact on people's lives. He explains why he needs to have this "direct impact":

> A pretty big part of it is my own religious beliefs, about the fact that we're not here only for ourselves, but we're here to serve others [*sic*]. And I've always felt that the direct impact I've had on others . . . really allowed me to feel that I've been able to serve others. I know that there are people that feel very comfortable serving others in kind of an indirect way.

Adams separates church and "being religious." Ultimately, both are connected to living a consistent philosophy of life that is taught in the church. He explains this philosophy:

> You know you think of the Ten Commandments and those things as far as being good to your neighbor. I think those [are] basic things, like being nice to your neighbor and be willing to help somebody else out who needs some help and not just look out for yourself but look out for others as well.

Last, church also played a part in the social lives of young people. Two of the subjects I interviewed had met their spouses through church youth groups, and others grew up participating in youth group activities, activities that they recreated in their adult lives.

> Betty and I belonged to, I guess this is where I met her. We belonged to a youth fellowship [and] every Sunday night at 7 o'clock we'd go down to the church and this was our social life—playing games and refreshments. I was in the Congregational church and she was in the Methodist church. There were a lot of Sunday evenings, like we'd be dancing, that's what we would do, and I guess we've always been dancing until we got our new knees. And then, of course, when we came here, we got associated with this church, I think when we first moved here. Betty and I are both very active with the youth fellowships. When Dr. Holmes was here, we were both very active in that. And along with social events, church events, we haven't done, we go to church but we don't belong to any social groups now. I used to do a lot of work in the old fellowship hall with young people and putting on activities. I worked with the other parents. I think that's probably what made Thomas Hills a good place to live for us, because we have that close relationship with people today. (Driscoll)

The ministers were also significant to this social life.

> I hadn't been that involved until senior high, and we had two ministers, the Reverend Sterling White and the Reverend Hal Leaver. An indication of how important they were was that our son's name is Hal. And a son we had whose middle name is Sterling. So those two people formed our basic belief patterns and let us develop spiritually and socially too. (Wallace)

Ministers and pastors and church life provided a model of moral behavior that stood apart from the prejudices of family and nation. Many of the subjects in this study felt that the church and its version of moral life greatly influenced their thinking. The lessons of church life contradicted the societal trends of hatred against people of other nations and races. These lessons also provided a different perspective from the individualism that permeates American society. In addition, church provided the subjects in this research with opportunities to see their lives connected to the lives of others in their community. This not only allowed friendships and courtships to occur, it also allowed the beginning of social networks that are critical to civil society (Putnam, 1993).

Peers

It is reported that during early childhood, peers have a role in the developing patterns of cooperation and trust (Kohlberg, 1969, Piaget, 1950, and Riccards, 1973, in Silbiger, 1977, p. 182). Later in life, peers assist with the development of learning more complex roles of social order, such as leadership (Silbiger, 1977). In this research, the influence of peers was not mentioned that often. However, there were some interesting patterns regarding the practices of child-hood play, the significance of space to the development of peer groups, and the opportunity to grow up in a diverse community.

Many of the World War II generation grew up in neighborhoods with a fair amount of ethnic diversity. Rockford saw this as being valuable to having an "open mind." He said:

> I think people who grow up in an absolutely homogenous, socially isolated community have a hard time not being, to some degree, inherently narrow minded. You know, if you haven't experienced anything else, it's not even a criticism. You just haven't experienced it. You just don't know about these other things. When you grow up with a mixture of people, you begin to real-ize that people are different, he likes that, and he likes that, and I like the other thing.

Rockford's comments and the story told below by Michaels suggest that these early experiences with diversity helped shape an appreciation of minority viewpoints, an important democratic concept. Michaels's story is about going to dinner with his Italian neighbors. He said:

> There were other boys my age in the area . . . most of them from Italian fami-lies in my age group. It was kind of interesting. I got invited to their homes for dinner a couple of times. Was kind of revealing for me, a very different way of life. That I went into a small house and there would be five or six children in the family. And we would have spaghetti and so forth, an Italian meal. And they would serve wine, which my family were strict teetotalers. They didn't tell me it was wine. They asked me if I wanted a soda. And then the whole family watched as I took a large gulp and nearly strangled. I'd never had wine in my life. But it was interesting to see a different kind of family style, and yet one which was obviously working very well for them. They would tend to be some-times very loud and volatile, wave their arms to the point you think a murder was about to be committed, and then everything would be fine in a little while.

This opportunity to see other families functioning quite differently from one's own must also provide a lesson in the value of multiculturalism. At a very simplistic level, Michaels and the other subjects who grew up in diverse commu-nities must have learned that cultural differences are not necessarily problematic.

The structure of space in the community was also important to the lives of the subjects in this research and their associations with peers. Two of the subjects in this study talked about their town or village centers where they could "hang out."

The main street had a lot of shops and fun things to do. You could go down and have a soda and hang out and shop—that kind of thing. So kids actually hung out in that town after school, and then would have to take late buses out to the ten districts that fit into that. (Madison)

Witt talked about the value of having undeveloped lots on which to play:

There were at the end of the street beyond us probably six or eight undeveloped lots. . . . There was a big patch of sand down in there, I don't know where it came from, but we used to go down and play in that sand, and we also have our pickup baseball games down there too.

Having space to play and associate with peers was important to these people. It also meant that you were "never too far from home," as Forbes remarked.

Neighborhoods often played a role in who one played with or who was in what "gang." To Wallace, the "Vega Street boys" were the "center of my activities." Witt's "play group" was defined by his street. He said:

The neighborhood, so to speak, and even though I was in school in class with kids from five, six, seven, eight streets up this way and that way and so forth, by in large, our play group was just our own street. We didn't even reach over to the next street for the play group.

The neighborhoods were also where one went after school "because all the moms were home" (Wallace).

The World War II generation also talked about how they developed their own play life with their peers. They found or created their own entertainment. Forbes describes a circus he created with his playmates:

We had a little bit of a circus over here on the corner of Estes Road on a high knoll, and Mr. Hamitt had a four-legged chicken. Two legs come right off the back under the wing, and that was on display, and we had a cow, a horse, and that kind of thing. You had to make what you did—that's all.

Michaels also talked about being on his own:

I was active in the Boy Scouts. But that was, you were left on your own, which, in a way, was good for me. I did an awful lot of reading as a kid. I always have read anything I could get my hands on, all my life. That was an asset in a way. I look at my own children, they structure their lives so that they had a lot less time to read than I had. The television takes up a lot. But the number of activities they were involved in took an awful lot of their time. In my day, you had to find the use for the time yourself.

Of course, for Forbes, farm life did not leave a lot of time to entertain or to get into "trouble," especially when compared to those kids who "just went to school." He said:

> When we were on the farm, the farm sort of was a binder for us. We were busy enough, so there was no trouble. Things are different. These same persons who was [*sic*] growing up with me wasn't on a farm and just went to school. They could be in more trouble than you could shake a stick at, because they didn't have any place to go and take care of play.

There were, of course, some more direct peer influences. Simmons's friends helped her develop a more academic focus. Said Simmons:

> They were very, very academically inclined. So, although we got along very well, I was not very academically inclined. I was more the physical "let's go out and do something" kind of person. And they would go out and read books. It helped because I got to be a better student because I had them for friends.

In looking at the influence of peers, it is clear that peer life and the structure of community life were intertwined. First of all, the spaces in neighborhoods helped determine peer groups as well as opportunities for peer interaction. Vacant lots or main streets served as neighborhood gathering spots for these subjects as children. Keeping in the neighborhood also allowed other adults to help monitor children's play. The type of interaction these peers had was one in which they had control of what they did; they "made their own fun."

One's peers also influenced education. For Simmons, peers helped promote her interest and success in education, something she was less inclined to pursue.

Education

Verba, Scholzman, & Brady (1995) suggest that "education is the single best predictor of affiliation with a non-political organization. The other substantial effect comes from having been active in high school" (p. 432). The subjects in this book had varied educational experiences. These variations had to do with parents' and teachers' expectations and gender and program opportunities within the school. Often the influence of school life was evident through the individual relationships that developed between these subjects and their teachers and administrators. Almost all of these subjects were found to be active outside of the classroom.

Expectations

The value of learning and the continuation of a formal process of education was valued by all of the subjects in this book. As mentioned earlier, this value began in the home. "A lot of emphasis [was] on doing well, and I think that I had a lot to do more with my family than just with the school" (Thomas). Hedberg was one exception, in that her parents really did not expect her to continue her education. They saw education or school life as an opportunity for her to find a husband. She said:

> So I went to high school, and in high school my parents finally said just get her so that she can find a husband and she will be marriageable. Teach her how to cook, teach her how to iron, teach her how to sew, so that she won't be a burden to the husband. So my whole high school was to find a husband.

By the time she was in high school, Hedberg had been tracked into a system in which she could not succeed. She said:

> Then I went to high school, and I was in the dumb class. I always wondered about that though, because I wrote this paper where I compared Lincoln to Kennedy and the teacher gave me the smart class B. So! Well! And then I said well, if I can get the smart class B, why not a dumb class A? I mean, if I'm in a dumb class, why can't I have the grade that you would have given the dumb class kids. The paper was too good. Yeah, but I'm in a dumb class! So I deserve the dumb class A instead of smart class B. I'm smart, give me an A, just once give me an A. "No, you're going to get the B in the class." Thanks for nothing. . . . I never, ever, ever, ever, ever could get an A. It was like no matter what I did, I couldn't get an A.

Nicols also experienced educational tracking. She transferred into a public school from a Catholic school when she was in the ninth grade. She learned at an early age that "expectations were everything." Nicols said:

> It was an interesting situation for me in the sense that when I arrived there [the public school she was entering] that school was tracked. Vocational kids went to their own high school. There was a general education for people who were not going to go on, and then there were various divisions for the rest of the kids. You were tracked into a division and you stayed with those kids for all your classes. It was based on an IQ test or past performance or whatever. I got plunked down in the bottom middle of that group somewhere and was probably one of the few kids who regularly moved. Each year they would move me up a group and then properly junior year we did PSATs on which I did extremely well. I scored over 700 for the verbal part of it, so as I moved up one group at a time, they said "oh, she must be smart," and they put me in the top group from which I learned expectations are everything. The work

was no harder, the teachers were no better, there was no more work, grades were better.

The ability of Nicols not to take the school's determination of her capabilities seriously and Hedberg's ability to overcome the damage of her parents and the schools tracking system suggest that they both had some internal motivation. Both were able to overcome how these institutions thought about them; there was perhaps already something within them, either innate or learned, that taught them not to merely accept but to make things happen for themselves.

Another negative aspect of educational expectations involved issues of gender. Gender discrimination, like all such discrimination, is subtle. Hyland talked about how gender influenced how she was "steered" through the educational process:

> I look back at how I did in high school and my SAT scores and so forth. Knowing what I know now, it's [*sic*] probably an underachiever in what I ended up doing and where I went to college and studied and so forth. I probably could have gone, but it doesn't matter. I mean I could have done different things, but I didn't know about it. I was female at that point, and people didn't steer you in that direction anyway, and I made decisions really poorly.

Activities and opportunity

Activities outside of the classroom were very influential in the interpersonal growth of the subjects in this research. However, it was clear that opportunities for being active were different, depending on gender and on the schools themselves. Sports activities were an important part of the lives for many of the subjects in this study. Unfortunately, the opportunity to play sports greatly depended on gender.

> Back then, girls couldn't do a whole lot. I always wanted to play baseball, but I couldn't play baseball because I was a girl. You know, my brother was in Little League and all that. We used to go to all his games, but we never really did a lot. (Califano)

School did not provide equal opportunities, and Andrea knew that. Particularly, school "sports were boy oriented." Fortunately for Hyland, her sister had broken tradition, and in doing so, "made it okay" for her.

> My sister was a real tomboy. So that's really important probably because again in the time I grew up there was a real role distinction between males and females. The fact that she could bat a ball left handed and right handed and play as well as any boy made it okay for me. (Hyland)

For the boys, sports were always available, but for a few of the subjects in this research, there were expectations of a "balance" between athletics and other activities. For Forbes, these other activities involved farm work, and for Conners, these activities involved music.

> With my father I had to have a balance between music and the sports, so that I participated in all realms of the arts; I was in band, chorus, went to all-state chorus; was involved in all sports—we had championship basketball teams and baseball teams. And, I was in plays as a kid. (Conners)

Another commonality for these subjects was their participation in after-school or cocurricular activities. Many of these subjects saw these activities as being "fun" or what made school "worthwhile."

> What I remember back then was that I stayed after school virtually all the time, because that was the fun part of school. I remember having the feeling that, as an adolescent, that that was the thing that made school worthwhile. That just going to classes, if that's all I did, that would be boring. (Hyland)

The variety of opportunities for activities also varied according to school systems. Michaels grew up in an area that was expanding rapidly, and the school system was "limited." When Nicols switched into a public school, she saw it as "an opportunity to try some things that hadn't been available before" in her former Catholic school. Rockford went to a school that not only had a lot of activities but also allowed opportunities for students to plan and organize their own fun through fraternity and sorority life. This made for "more of a social life" separate from the school's.

> Each of or almost all of the fraternities and sororities would put on social functions, and we would have dances throughout the seasons. There might be eight to ten dances where the fraternity or sorority and, in a couple of cases, the sorority put on a formal dance where several of them got together. It was held at the big hotel. They raised the money themselves, they hired the band, hired the hall, paid the expenses, and shared any profits. Whichever organization kept the profits so there was . . . that tended to make a lot more of a social life, and that social life was independent of the school system. (Rockford)

Teachers and adult caring

Adults did play a significant role in the school life of these students. They were able to show students that they did matter, and they often helped students in their educational and career life. Hall (1914, as cited in Hyman, 1959) first noticed the waning influence of parents compared to teachers. Many of the subjects in this research mentioned specific teachers and how these teachers had influenced them.

> In the early days in high school, I would say [I was] maybe a B student. . . . School was hard, not easy, for me. School was hard and yet I had . . . I remember there was a science teacher when I was in eleventh grade that took a real liking to me. And he spent a lot of time with me that year because I was struggling. And I really think because of him that kind of nurtured my attitudes about going into nurse's training, because he really did—he fired something up. He really fired up science for me and the rest of it. (Constantino)

Feeling valued by adults outside of the family was important to these subjects. The fact that this occurred within an educational setting by adults who valued education promoted the academic careers of many of the subjects.

> I think I was fortunate in having some great teachers, some of whom took an interest in me because I was a good student and there weren't any guidance counselors. [They] undertook to coach me how to apply to college and that sort of thing. Teachers coming to talk to my parents about it and helped the whole family with the whole process because it was totally new to us. (Michaels)

The teachers also made up for the lack of resources or educational opportunities. At the very least, they tried.

> I was an athlete, but I wasn't a student. At that time Mike Lucas wasn't that worried about it. If we wanted the time off to go pheasant hunting, he would let you go, but when he found out that two of us wanted to go to college, which was something back then . . . [he] said, "the two of you guys want to go to college, I'll tell you what." Mike says, "I just got married" and says "you come down to my house and camp on Bedford Lake and Mabell's going to visit and I'll show you fellas. I'll give you a short course in chemistry." So here's Andy and I getting ready to go. He's going to Illinois, and I'm going to Cornell. So his idea was to give something as a catalyst to make this experiment work better. So here's what he did. He said "you fellas need a little brushin' up." So he brought us down to talk to us really, didn't amount to nothing, but he was going to bake some cupcakes. So he put them in the oven, and he said, now I'll add the baking soda so they'll rise see. Well, they fell and they had a hole in the middle. He put strawberry jam in the middle and we eat 'em, in a blackened room, you know. And Mabell came home and almost threw us all out. That was Mike. He was just afraid that he hadn't taught us enough. (Forbes)

These teachers also provided emotional support and adult concern for students who lacked such concern from family or peers.

I was a good girl . . . lackluster is one of the words that comes to me as far as coming up through school. I remember in junior high I got used to the music teacher there, and I remember one phone conversation her saying, "Oh Anne I wish you had more friends or a best friend or something." Those three years were pretty void. There again, I was also close to, close to the math teacher. I hated math and algebra, and interestingly enough or amazingly enough, the algebra teacher took to me. She had no children of her own, invited me out to her house on a weekend. I can't remember if I stayed over, I think I did; they were out on Long Island, so they took me to Jones Beach, and so forth, you know. So I appealed to adults; I didn't appeal to my peers. (Sharpe)

Of course, teachers were not the only adults who played significant roles in these subjects' lives. In fact, many of them mentioned how certain adults had helped them out. The help and attention that teachers and other adults provided was often the reason these subjects said they chose to be involved.

There are also people that really helped me along the way in terms of dealing with that disease [diabetes]. I remember in college. . . . This guy was just the most common, caring guy, and I'll always remember him. The guy was about 4 foot 10 and his name was Bill Brooks, and he was just a terrific, caring person, and I always felt like, well, if I was having problems . . . he was always there. It's people like that that I think also influenced me in terms of my help with other people. When I decided what to do for graduate school, I remember being very proud of telling him of what I was doing. . . . It was as if I was telling him, I kind of have seen how you have cared for me and cared for other students, probably all the students here, and its kind of the way I'm moving in terms of my own life. (Thomas)

All of these adults were, however, identified for one quality—caring. When I asked Smith about why he believed some teachers were memorable, he offered the following:

Because of personality, because of caring for kids, I guess. I mean, as I remember them, being involved with their students. You never had the feeling that it was a nine-to-three job. That the teacher was there when you got there in the morning and was there as long as you wanted them in the afternoon.

College

While the expectation of attaining a college degree was strong for this group, there were generational differences. College was not the expectation for Forbes, who grew up in the 1930s on a farm. However, there were a number of adults who cared about him and who encouraged him to go on to college. One of them got him to "see if college was for [him] or not." Forbes said:

Albert Merchant went to what they call a winter course school. Albert was my neighbor up the road. . . . So he said, you know, you want to do something to see if college is for you or not, go to Cornell during the winter. You go in November, you stay until February, short course they call it. I think that was the most influence on my life . . . and my wife too. She was a smart person to know that if I wanted to do it you could do it. So by going to Cornell for this winter course, I took agriculture subjects and nutrition subjects and genetics. I got really interested in genetics. . . . I think that short course was probably the breaking point from high school to college.

Getting a college education was expensive, and different circumstances enabled many of the subjects in this study to pursue higher education. For the World War II generation, it was the GI bill, which allowed many who served in World War II to go to college and heightened the expectation that college was not just for the rich. The baby boom generation, for example, seemed to have higher expectations of attending college, but again, the financial aspects of college life were critical to where one went. Nicols was able to go to college because of a specific program at Johnston College, where she came face-to-face with privilege. This experience led her to a "great respect for the system that allows people to rise to whatever level they are capable of." Nicols said:

That was an interesting experience for me to realize as I grow older I am a graduate of Johnston College, which happens to be in my hometown, and if you could get in, they would let you live at home and pay one-quarter tuition. That was perceived then and probably is still perceived as being one of the best women's colleges and a good college in the United States. Here I was the young lady whose parents never got out of high school with people whose parents had advanced degrees, had a lot of money. As I looked around, I said, okay these people have had experiences and opportunities that I didn't have. Are they better than me? The answer was no, they are not better than me. They had different opportunities just like my dad. Had he had different opportunities, he would have been a different person than he is, because intelligence and got-to-stick-to-it entrepreneurship aren't given to you, they get born in you, so he was a good example of the fact that all people are created equal in the U.S. of A. I have great respect for the system that allows people to rise to whatever level they are capable of.

While education played a significant role in the socialization of the subjects in this study, its influence was mediated by societal norms of gender roles, economic opportunities to pursue education, educational practices, and individuals who work in the schools or who live in the community and take an interest in young people. Often it is these individual adults who modeled the subjects' future involvement in civil society.

Organizations: Scouting and the YMCA

Two other organizations that were mentioned by several subjects were scouting and the YMCA, which provided opportunities to learn about responsibility. Each summer at a YMCA camp, Witt took on progressively more responsible positions. As mentioned before, Wallace saw scouting as an activity that taught about the real consequences of one's actions. He said:

> And I think you also learn if kinda for every freedom you have there is incumbent responsibility. Scouts—well—they teach you that. It's probably the whole program. And it kind of gets ingrained into ya. And you're also learning if you're going off to summer camp and you do something crazy you can end up wallowing in mud in a swamp because you didn't hit the last compass point. So if you know how to do it right, you avoid going through the muddy lagoon, and if you don't you track through the muddy lagoon. There's consequences for actions, and you learn it fairly rapidly.

Media

The role of media is particularly important in understanding issues related to identity and public problem solving. Media, and its evolution from radio to television, carries with it different perspectives or modes of learning (Postman, 1985). These modes shape how the subjects in this research understood their roles in public life. In addition, the ability to be engaged in public problem solving is dependent on knowledge of community issues. Therefore, the daily routines of paying attention to national and international news should be and were important to the subjects in this study. For the subjects who were interviewed in depth, the form and content of news, particularly along generational lines and gender, did provide some interesting differences.

Generational differences and media

Television was not around for the World War II generation. Their media was the radio or, for Witt, short wave.

> My father was very interested in what was going on in this country and in the world, and we were not unique or alone in this, and in fact, I've heard my wife say the same thing that during the war years, particularly the noon meal was eaten in silence while the news was on the radio—the war news. My father had been an amateur radio operator in the days when all radio was Morse code, so he was and in fact had been in the signal corp as a consequence in the First World War. He was very good with code and when the war first started before we were involved, he would turn on the short wave and pick up the

news dispatches that were coming from Europe and the correspondence which in those early years were being transmitted in the clear so he could sit and read those dispatches right from the code. (Witt)

As a media, radio required more active participation. Witt talked about how radio required imagination. He said:

There was no television in those days, either. It was radio, and when you listened to radio, whether it was Edgar Bergen and Charlie McCarthy or a soap opera, and the soaps started first on radio, why you had to imagine or envision the scene you were hearing which was a form of stimulation too.

Gender and media

In reflecting on the significance of media in their lives, some subjects recognized the impact of radio and television on their views of gender roles. Hyland had this to say when I asked her what she meant by describing herself as a "backstage" person, or someone who does not take on highly visible leadership roles:

That's a good question.... I take it because it is more comfortable with who I am, but why is it more comfortable with who I am? Part of the answer is, who knows. But I find it fascinating that when I do go back and watch Nick at Night or some of the old shows that were part of my culture growing up, and that was the female role. Very often, you didn't really have female superstars. You had a female at best if she were a heroine or whatever was in support of a hero. If you look at any of the sitcoms, the wife was the supporter of the husband. I mean that even if we were laughing at the husband's foibles, the wife would be there kind of making everything okay, but in a way that wouldn't hurt his pride.... There's a lot that I think is interesting watching those shows. Perhaps how, not that they created, not that television necessarily created that influence in my life; I think it was more a mirror of how things were.... If you listen to the music even of that time, a lot of the music, maybe to some degree it's still true, [it] had to do with a woman's identity being tied up with the man she married or whose ring she was wearing or whatever.... This was before Betty Friedan and *The Feminine Mystique* and women's lib. I was kind of growing up in the midst of that change. My childhood was before that, and my adolescence and young adulthood was kind of in the midst of that.

ADULT SOCIALIZATION TO CIVIL SOCIETY

Adult socialization has been underdeveloped as a research area (Sigel & Hoskin, 1977, p. 259), but it is critically important as leadership skills are often developed and refined within adult social institutions based on individual experiences (Renshon, 1990, p. 317). Riley, Foner, Hess, and Toby (1969, as cited in Sigel & Hoskin, 1977) describe adult socialization:

Successful socialization beyond childhood involves a continual search for the delicate adjustment between the individual's internalized values and definitions and his specific judgments of the behaviors and attitudes appropriate to each new role situation. On the one hand, he implements his basic values in a specific situation; on the other, each new situation contributes to his basic value pattern as he generalizes the pattern (or modifies or reinforces it) to cover the new specific applications. (p. 261)

The influences that had an impact on the attitudes, values, and practices of civic life for these subjects included a historical event, World War II, their families of procreation, their careers, and the community they live in today, the Town of Bedford. The subjects mentioned several aspects of their community that now seemed relevant to civic life, including suburban growth, supporting children, community identity, social problems, and gender. These will be discussed later, but for now the following section will provide an example of how history can shape the perspectives of citizens.

War

The World War II generation frequently mentioned the impact of the war on their awareness of world events and their need to take responsibility for national interests. Often the whole family followed the war news on the radio. While it is somewhat speculative, it is also likely that such an awareness of national concerns helped these subjects internalize some sense of national purpose. This reflects what Wallace felt was a generational shift away from "pro what I call 'we'" He said:

And I think there's been a kind of a change in philosophy if you have the term. Most of us born in that same era [World War II] that were teenagers before the sixties generally were pro what I call "we." . . . And then in the sixties, I think there was a movement that where the "I" became much more important. And so I see a general trend away from volunteerism. It's what I do has to have immediate value to me. Rather than putting off my needs for a greater cause. You're aware also that of course happened generally. We were brought up in a we era, and that has set patterns in our lives to be associated with.

Family of Procreation

As was mentioned earlier, family life was highly valued by these people. Their ties to their families often put them into contact with and participation in the voluntary associations that made up the community. As mentioned earlier, many individuals became involved in the school board through their concerns for their children's education. Some were involved with sports organizations because of their children. In all cases, their involvement began with self-interest around the family of procreation but over time became more of a general concern for all of the children of the community.

Daloz et al. (1996) also suggest that "some form of responsibility to particular others, or work that corresponds to the challenges and joys that marriage and children can bring, fosters the development of the self-knowledge, perspective, and passion that nourishes committed citizenship" (p. 51).

Career

Another influence in adult socialization is work life. I asked each of these subjects about their work lives. They had a tendency to trace their experiences or the history of places they had worked to the kinds of work they had done. Two particular themes emerged from their comments, which included gender and opportunities for contributing to society and how certain jobs had stronger links to the community.

In talking about their careers, many of the female subjects in this research expressed how gender had influenced their choices. Sharpe found that gender determined that she had to work in an office. "The idea was that I would go and get some training in agriculture, so then I could work in the office of some agriculture whatever, because you know at that time that's where a woman went." This denied her certain opportunities, so she had to find alternatives.

Family care also was assumed to be the responsibility of the women in the families, and, again, that limited their professional opportunities. Califano had a background in teaching, but she assumed that when she had a family she would stay at home. "We started a family, and I had no intention of working anyway, so I stayed home," she said.

While Califano felt that it was her decision to stay home, this expectation and limitations for women in the world of work may have led to their need to be involved in public life in other ways. These women were highly capable and well educated, yet their opportunities to work full time were limited by their family responsibilities and by the work opportunities available to them. Given these limitations, their involvement in voluntary associations may be considered an expression of their need to contribute to society in ways other than through the workplace or their need for growth. Nicols is a good example. She stayed at home to raise her family but found opportunities for growth through her work in the community. She said:

> The opportunities I have had through volunteer work have been real growth experiences. When you get involved in the kinds of things I've done, you have

opportunities to take courses, to go to workshops, to go to conventions, and you learn not only what you need to know to help blend the organization you're involved in, but you learn things that help you to grow. I have had interesting opportunities through volunteering.

Clearly some of these individuals did not see these expectations as restrictions. Califano made a conscious choice to stay home and to not use her education as a trained teacher. However, her expectations of her role in the world, especially in regard to family life, determined this choice. In some sense, it was not really a choice. The expectation of her role was determined by her socialization. The most powerful expression of socialization is when the societal norms of the many public and private roles that we play are internalized as matter of fact.

The second theme that emerged from these discussions was that what one did for work could influence one's relationship to the community. This was particularly true for people who work or who had worked in education. It is interesting to note that eleven out of the nineteen subjects interviewed were involved as professional educators at one point in their lives. Smith talked about how his responsibilities in the public schools led to community involvement. He said:

I guess part of being involved in public education in the community, there is a certain amount of social involvement, PTA and Rotary and chaperoning the dances and that kind of thing. So community involvement has, to a greater or less degree, been a part of what I've done.

Michaels, as mentioned earlier, also suggested that his involvement in the community was based on a "natural inclination and a lifetime of [work in] public education."

While work life or the choice of what one chooses to do may be already determined by gender, personality, aptitude, and interest—factors established during childhood and adolescence—the practice of work still is significant to the social and political contexts in which one is placed. The work contexts are shown here to influence civic involvement in important ways.

Community Today

The civic life in the Town of Bedford is also significant to adult socialization. The history of the community and its public practices of community problem solving influence who gets involved and how. The subjects in this research discussed how the community developed around concerns for education and child rearing. They also talked about the need for a greater sense of community identity, a community practice of denying social problems, and how gender still influences public behavior.

Suburban growth and child care

As revealed by the subjects in this study, the history of the growth in the Town of Bedford also shaped the opportunities for involvement in civil society. Three different groups settled the area. The first was made up of the rural farmers who came to the area in the late 1700s to mid-1800s. Forbes and his family best represent this group, and his stories speak to the life of the area before the growth of industry in Thomasville. The second group was composed of those who worked for the railroads. This group probably represents what Bueller calls the "lake residents," who seemed to pass down property from one generation to the next. The third group was made up of highly educated, well-paid employees of various companies that grew in Thomasville. It was this last group that has become the more dominant in terms of involvement in community organizations today.

This last group came to the area for jobs in industry, engineering, and research. It represented a highly educated, well-paid population. Since many of these people had also come to this community to raise their children, there was among them a high value of education and support for the schools. The shared mission of child raising and educational support encouraged the growth of community involvement. Rockford describes this time:

> The population had absolutely mushroomed in the years between 1946 and 1957. With the post-war period, you had a huge influx of people coming out from the research laboratories, the atomic power laboratory, and from downtown ME [Montauk Electric], and you ended up with a lot of very well-educated people moving into the community. This is the core, that group that is so community minded. Because we had a very high Ph.D. population, these people expected their children would go on and get advanced degrees, so they promoted the schools. We've had a very strong interest and support for schools in this area. It has been a community, as I say, of active participants. The community people had all kinds of advisory committees going on, so everybody was doing something.

This was a time when whole neighborhoods were developing, and people got to know each other while they shared similar life-course issues around raising children and forming community life. "We all moved in within six months of each other, and we formed a close alliance over the years. We're kinda like family, even though, you know, we came from all different spectrums" (Wallace).

According to Simmons, who arrived in the community in the 1970s, this commonality of coming in from other places eliminated problems of fighting between families in more tradtional, stable communities. She said: "I grew up in a small town; you don't get the feeling that, I don't know, there's no infighting. There's no animosity. Your great grandmother didn't do something that offended somebody."

The community and, in particular, the subjects in this research shared a concern for young people. This shared concern was part of what brought people together and connected them to each other. Thomas said that maybe it was because he is on the school board, but "a lot of people [here] care about kids, care about community, care about their neighborhood." It was felt that school was the center or the "only binding force" (Michaels) in the community. Thomas felt that school was a major focal point for those in the community who had children. He said:

> I feel that the schools in this area are a focal point for a lot of activities for kids, and therefore, for their parents. But 50 percent, more than 50 percent, 55 percent of our community, don't have any kids in school. So those people tend to be part of the community when it comes to their church, but in terms of the community at large, there isn't really a coming together of all the different age groups, and different levels where people are at. You know, the empty nest group, senior citizens, young parents, young singles, young marrieds, and kids—because nothing kind of brings it all together.

Community identity

Providing a focal point for the community was a common goal for many of the subjects in this study. Part of the concern was caused by a lack of "identity" in the community. Smith said: "We're a community struggling to find an identity." Mostly this had to do with the availability of common space to "come and visit." Smith explains the success of the Rotary's Apple Pie Festival: "One of the beauties of that, apart from the pie, is that people come and sit and talk and visit. People don't come and talk and visit in this town. There's no place to do it." He compares this to the frequent use of public space as social space in his own hometown.

These gatherings were not simply to be able to see everybody together as much as they were to give community members a sense of themselves as belonging to the community. Bueller thought that it was more likely to occur in a rural rather than in an urban area. He explained this sense of community:

> I think they're close as far as knowing your neighbor and some things like that and being involved in helping your neighbor out and, again, doing things strictly because it is going to benefit the community as far as benefiting themselves.

Of course, Bueller represents more of the lake resident community that has been more stable and that has been around much longer. Michaels's experience in his neighborhood led him to believe that this sense of community has declined. While it has been "very stable," people "don't visit back and forth." He believes that we are more isolated from one another because we are "less dependent upon our neighbors for companionship."

It was also frequently mentioned that this was a problem because the community, and more specifically, the school, is "sprawled over two counties, what four townships. There is no governmental entity. Thomas Hills or Bedford Lake are not any kind of organized municipalities; they're postal districts by definition" (Michaels).

This lack of community identity provides a direction for some of these organizations. The local Rotary Club saw this as one of its key missions. Smith talks about how Rotary works as a "community builder." He said:

> For several years now, Rotary's had a Christmas tree over on the corner. We tried for many years to turn that into a community event where people would come and sing and so on. We never could pull it off until the last two years, but that's a community builder. I think of it as a sidewalk. Not a concrete sidewalk, but a social sidewalk that brings the community together.

Somehow the lack of public space and the failure of community members to have a sense of belonging to the community was perceived by the subjects in this study as a problem. In their work, they have come together with likeminded individuals to try to change this.

Social problems

Many of the subjects also felt that this community was in a "chronic state of denial" (Sharpe) regarding the various social problems of drugs, alcohol, and especially poverty. Poverty was "well hidden," according to Hedberg. Bueller realized these problems primarily because of his sister. He said:

> Being that my sister is a social worker in the high school, I do have an opportunity . . . you know, you do think you are living in the perfect lifestyle here and all that stuff goes on in Thomasville and Easton, you don't experience it here, but being that she is a social worker, she has told me some things that holy cow, unreal. I mean you're talking girls eleven years old being pregnant and stuff like that, broken families. You hear those stories and you think, wow Thomas Hills/Bedford Lake School system, you got to be kidding. That was a shock.

Michaels talked about some of the social problems in the community, and that the community had responded by creating the HSC organization through the combined efforts of the Rotary Club, the town, and the school. As was suggested earlier, however, it came about through the realization of problems in the school.

Many of the subjects in this study were involved with the schools at the time. They were more aware of these community problems and helped create the HSC. Again, in this community, school life and raising children did seem to provide opportunities for a common mission or vision of community.

Gender

Gender issues were often mentioned by the women in this study. Within this community, gender influenced how individuals acted within public life. Simmons mentioned that this was true in her grandmother's time, her mother's time, and even today. She said:

> Definitely, I don't think there are very many people in this town, women, in this town, who want to be known as having opinions. It's appalling to me that they will all sit there and be wishy-washy. And I can't do that. I'm sure they all think I'm terrible, but I just cannot take that. And there are very few women in public life in this town. Matter of fact, the only women who are in public life in this town are on the boards I'm on—interesting.

CONCLUSIONS

The subjects in this book did demonstrate some patterns in their early and adult socialization that seem related to their involvement in the many voluntary associations within civil society. However, these patterns of socialization are highly complex and reflect significant historical arrangements associated with social, economic, and cultural changes. Yet despite these historical differences, there were still certain aspects of a number of mediating institutions that were held in common by many, if not all, of the subjects in this study.

The family was, perhaps, the most critical mediating institution, as it set the tone for the valuing of social life. The families of the subjects in this research were particularly attentive to the needs of children. In a sense, the social interactions of the family between parent and child and between siblings were valued, which may explain why many of the subjects value the social interaction of voluntary associations.

The child-rearing patterns in these families also promoted a sense of self-reliance. If the family is the first model of organizational life for children, then these subjects learned very early that they had to take responsibility, and that they had to follow strict guidelines of behavior. Many of the subjects of the research had to take on very real, immediate responsibilities for the successful functioning of the family. Often this involved hard work. These experiences promoted taking charge, for oneself and perhaps for the well-being of the communal associations that one enters into as an adult.

The intellectual life of the family also played a key part of the socialization influences significant to civil society. The family dinner table was the place where debates and discussions took place. These discussions provided the subjects of this study with discursive examples of how to argue. As adults, they probably used these examples to provide a pattern of how public problems should be resolved on the boards on which they served.

The parents of these subjects, regardless of their education, also had a tendency to value learning, and they set an example for these subjects by keeping up with national and international news. The parents were role models not only because of their awareness of what was happening in the community and in the world, but because they also took an active stance in doing something about resolving social problems. This could explain why these subjects were more aware and more attentive to the needs of their community.

School and community life also presented the subjects in this study with adults outside of their family who cared about them and encouraged them to go on with their education. Many of the subjects referred to these adults as they tried to explain their own tendencies for volunteering to support the youth in their community today. Certainly the raising of children from a community perspective was a major influence and motivation for involvement in many voluntary associations.

Another commonality among these subjects was the access to public space. The subjects in this research grew up in communities where there was frequent interaction with other community members. These interactions occurred while shopping, playing, working, or being entertained. Frequency of contact with others within the community promotes a sense of belonging to a community and an expectation of social interaction as an adult, a value that many of the subjects in this study tried to replicate in their community today.

Lastly, church life was significant because it provided an alternative view of morality that contradicted the prejudice and hatred prevalent in family life and in society in general. Subjects mentioned how the influence of this perspective enabled them to challenge the negative views they had learned from their family about people different from themselves. This may help explain the openness of many of the subjects in this study. Church teachings also provided a context or perspective for these subjects. They were taught that their lives were tied to a larger purpose, to all humans as creations of God. This may help explain their ability to see self-interest within a broader context of public life.

While all of these mediating structures helped shape how the subjects in this book understood their roles as citizens, certain historical transitions also influence these mediating structures and make the whole process of socialization that much more complex. Economic changes determined the stability of neighborhoods in which these subjects grew up and then formed as adults.

This stability is particularly significant, since it allowed these subjects to live in communities where people knew each other and where there was a shared sense of community.

Cultural values relating to gender often determined the roles and choices that women had available to them. In some cases, this may have actually encouraged women to be more involved in voluntary associations when work life did not allow them to contribute to the welfare of their communities. This should not be misconstrued as an argument to keep women out of the workplace. Many of the male subjects in this study were better able to contribute to their communities due to their work experience and the networks that it provided.

There are also dramatic changes in how our society entertains itself. While in the past entertainment was a social endeavor that relied on neighbors and other community members, today entertainment is something we can do at home. We can play games, we can watch movies, and we can even shop without having to leave home. Considering the frequency of social contact by these subjects in their communities of orientation, it is clear that this transformation may have a negative impact on participation in civil society.[2]

Some other changes mentioned by the subjects in this study were the practice of play and the valuing of family life. The subjects of the World War II generation discussed how play was something one made up with one's peers. The baby boom generation described their earlier play this way, but as they went on in school, play became organized by adults. Those baby boomers who had children described their children's play today as being totally organized by adults. This progression suggests that children are being socialized in a way that they depend on others to determine the rules of play and the negotiation of conflict. The implication of this for citizenship is obvious. If children learn to play only in situations where rules are externally defined, then they may continue to look for external control in their adult lives. Instead of being democractic citizens responsible for negotiating the rules for civil society, they will rely on an external authority such as the state or corporate interests to determine the rules for their community.

Lastly, some of the subjects in this study felt that there has been a shift of values away from family life and toward material gain. Hyland remarked on a point her husband made, that in affluent communities, "people are really struggling to kind of bring in more income to have more things than . . . maybe there isn't the time to supervise." If familial attention to children is the beginning point for the valuing of social interaction, and it is declining, then participation in civil society will also decline.

The interrelationship among values systems, economic changes, and social life in general made it clear that socialization to civil society is a highly complex process. To understand why the subjects in this study choose to be engaged in the voluntary associations that make up civil society, it is necessary to understand their life histories and the unique historical developments that shaped those life histories. While not negating the possibility of other psychological factors such as personality influencing this process, it is clear that historical patterns of social, economic, and cultural change shape the environments in which any pattern of citizenship can take place. For the model of citizens we studied, certain factors were critically important. Were parents and older adults in the community attentive and supportive to young people? Did parents and these other adults provide young people with opportunities to take on responsibilities, responsibilities that had real consequences for the child and for the family of the child? Did the notion of taking on responsibility factor into the school environment? Were teachers and other adults encouraging young people to pursue their education? Did the neighborhood have some stability and allow for the day-to-day contact of community members? Did the church play any role in the lives of young people? Did the church challenge or support the prejudicial assumptions of traditional communities? How did all of these mediating structures fit into the civic careers of the individuals who make up and play key roles in the various voluntary associations of civil society?

Chapter 7

Discussion and Conclusions

In trying to understand how citizens are socialized to take an active role in the various voluntary associations that comprise civil society, complex relations between value systems, economic change, and social life must be discerned. The model of citizenship described in this book and the subjects' narratives have provided evidence for how socialization and the varying agents of socialization (i.e., family, school, work, church, and communities of orientation) might be able to promote an active citizenry that recognizes self-interest within a broader context of public good. Such citizenship, it has been argued, is essential to the generation of civic responsibility (Derber, 1996) and to the possibility of collective action within a democratic state (Putnam, 1993).

This book has served two purposes: (1) to describe those individuals who are engaged in these voluntary associations and who demonstrate enlightened self-interest in this engagement in community affairs and (2) to explore the various agents of socialization that may have led to such engagement. This focus has yielded results that relate to previous research and strengthened the focus on community life rather than on political society.

Why individuals become engaged in the voluntary associations of civil society was explained in this study by examining the civic careers of model citizens. The notion of civic careers proves useful since explaining such behavior requires an understanding of human development as it relates to a specific individual's natural capacities and the opportunities and environments that surround that individual. To understand an individual's civic career, it is necessary to have a descriptive knowledge of that person's past, beginning with family life and continuing into the experiences of adulthood. During childhood, adolescence, and early adulthood, the individual develops and internalizes underlying value systems that are significant to future learning (Sigel, 1989, p. ix). However, these early developments can only lay the foundations on which future

151

civic behavior can be understood. Development related to civic involvement occurs into adulthood as new roles and tasks are taken on within a variety of social and political contexts (Steckenrider & Cutler, 1989, p. 57).

In exploring the civic careers of this particular model of citizen, this book has many parallels to a study by Clausen (1993). He was able to use and extend longitudinal data developed at the University of California at Berkeley to explore the development of a number of individuals born in the 1920s. Clausen (1993) was able to identify significant aspects of human development and how they relate to a person becoming a "competent" (p. xiii) adult and an effective, satisfied human being (p. 2). In Clausen's book, *American Lives*, he argues that *planful competence* is a key determinant to the life course. He describes the life course as follows:

> In summary, the life course entails the negotiation by an active, self-aware person of a set of potentially available roles that are interlinked, many of which are concurrent. Each person makes choices governing the importance of various roles to which he or she commits some level of allegiance for some period of time, accumulating experiences that influence future development and change. (Clausen, 1993, p. 17)

The idea of *planful competence* means that the individual has self-knowledge, certain abilities and controls (Clausen, 1993, p. 19). "It entails knowing: something about one's intellectual abilities, social skills, and emotional responses to others; one's interests and developing them; and about available options and thinking about how to take advantage of or expand them" (ibid.).

Clausen's findings reveal that individuals who "by late adolescence have a realistic view of their abilities, know in a general way what they want, and consider the consequences of their choices are more likely to make smooth transitions and adaptations and to remain satisfied with their decisions" (ibid.). Clausen describes the three main components of planful competence as dependability, intellectual involvement, and self-confidence (p. 16).

In this study, similar elements or qualities were found in these model citizens. The subjects in this research learned at an early age that they were depended upon by their family and by the members of the many organizations to which they belonged throughout their childhood and adolescence. The family life and the values of the model citizens in this research were also marked by the value of learning and by engagement in the intellectual life of the world around them. These model citizens also developed a sense of confidence in their abilities through the encouragement of adults within their families and through their experiences in a variety of voluntary organizations in schools and in civil society in general. In a sense, the parallels between this research and Clausen's (1993) work suggest that the promotion of citizen engagement in civil society requires no more than paying attention to human development and the influences that lead to confident, competent, reliable, and intellectually engaged citizens. To a great degree, such development begins very early in the family.

The family is perhaps the first and most prominent agent of socialization, since it begins to shape how individuals see the world. Family life sets the moral foundation on which future experiences and influences take shape (Sears, Maccoby, & Levin, 1957, as cited in Davies, 1977, p. 165). For many of the subjects in this study, the value of family life and the attention parents gave to their children most likely encouraged a world view in which these subjects had an internalized sense of control (Davies, 1977, pp. 165–166) and a perception of the world as being a trustworthy rather than a hostile place (Davies, 1977, p. 169).

Clausen's (1993) study also found several significant influences of family life that were quite similar to the experiences of many of the subjects in this study. These experiences of family life included family harmony, strict parenting, and valuing of intellectual matters. Clausen found that "family harmony" can influence a young person's self-esteem and her or his tendency to become a "responsible adolescent." In this study, such harmony or quality of family life was often present. Subjects suggested that family always came first, and they talked about their close relations to parents and peers.

Clausen found that "one of the strongest predictors of adolescent planful competence for boys was having parents rated 'overdemanding'" (1993, p. 526). Many of the subjects in this study described this notion of having overdemanding or strict parents. Their parents set clear limits of behavior and reinforced accommodation of these limits.

According to Clausen, the "valuing of intellectual matters, having wide interests, and being open to new experiences" (1993, p. 524) is also significant to planful competence. These values were clearly a part of the subjects' family lives in this study as well. Discourse at family meals and family discussions in general, described by many of the subjects in this study, may have also led to an interest in political life (Verba, Schlozman, & Brady, 1995, p. 436).

Of course, there were other relevant family practices that had a more direct influence on the civic capacity of the subjects in this research. Parents and older siblings of many subjects in this book acted as role models for involvement in social and community organizations. This modeling of social participation in families has been argued to influence children's future orientation toward social participation (Anderson, W. A., 1946, as cited in Barber, 1980, p. 61). Another family related influence was the organization of children's play.

A number of the subjects discussed their play as children. They mentioned that they used to create and organize their own play, while today's children typically interact with peers in play settings controlled by adults. The ability to create the rules by which social interactions take place is an important aspect of group interaction and democratic life. These changes in the practice of play might suggest an overall deterioration in the development of skills necessary to organize local public life around mutual interests.

Of course, for citizens to take any kind of an active role in local public life, they must believe that they can have some influence or some sense of individual competence. Clausen (1993) found that "an adolescent's competence by the end of the high school years—planful competence—influences the scheduling of the major social roles later occupied, the stability of role performance, and the person's attainment and life satisfaction over much of the life course" (p. 18). For the subjects in this book, much of this sense of competence was supported by the schools and by the involvement of community members in their lives.

Education provided opportunities for leadership development. Many of the subjects in this study actively participated in school life, which is said to enhance the "propensity for activity" later in life (Almond & Verba, 1963). However, education also provided these subjects with caring adults other than parents with whom they could foster relationships and receive some of the attention that some of them were lacking at home or with their peers. Having adults in the community who cared about them or who took an interest in them was one of the most frequently mentioned explanations for why these subjects chose to get involved as adults.

Education also encourages openness and rational debate over public issues (Hyman, 1959, p. 145). While these subjects did indeed have specific norms of public debate that required them to be open and rational, it is difficult to discern whether or not education is the source of these values; moreover, these values most likely result from a combination of factors related to family, peers, and education. Class may also be a contributing factor and, for the most part, all of these subjects came from working-class or middle-class families.

One factor often overlooked in the literature was the community of orientation or the neighborhood in which these subjects grew up. The communities in which the subjects in this study grew up had multiple opportunities for association; they had defined areas in which people shopped, worked, and played. Often children had open public spaces within neighborhoods, so that they played with and knew many of the people in their neighborhoods. These neighborhoods provided support with child raising due to their stability. People moved into these neighborhoods with the intention of living there to raise their families. They were immediately tied to the success and prosperity of their communities. These ties and commitments to a place allowed people to know one another and to develop the networks to make their lives manageable, particularly in regard to child care.

Of course, not all of the subjects in this study had the support of adults and family members. As Clausen found, "case histories can be deceiving" (1993, p. 43).

A dramatic instance of a child's overcoming an extremely pathological family setting and becoming a competent, delightful person may almost convince us that early child rearing makes little difference. A systematic testing of that hypothesis, however, requires statistical data. As will be seen, most often a pathological family setting leads to unhappy outcomes in adult life. (Clausen, 1993, p. 43)

Hedberg especially and, to some degree, others in this study did grow up in a poor family setting. She was perhaps the most extreme, since she came from a family environment that informed her that she was unwanted and worthless. Yet Hedberg did overcome this early family influence to become an important member of her community today.

Hedberg's ability to overcome her childhood may reflect an innate response to fight rather than flight. She may have had the capacity to resist the negative influences of her early life and to make the most of positive influences. For Hedberg, these influences included the church and later, as an adult, the voluntary associations themselves.

Church life and its socialization effects were also quite prominent for a number of other subjects in this study. While the involvement of these subjects in youth groups and church-sponsored activities did teach the leadership skills and provide access to networks necessary for involvement in civil society and political life, these subjects also felt that church provided them with an alterenative view of the world.

This was significantly important to how Hedberg valued herself and others. Church taught her that her parents' prejudicial perspectives of others were not universally held, and that maybe their ideas about her were also inaccurate. This experience of learning different perspectives and becoming critical of values is imporant to civil society and public life. Certain values of intolerance do not allow for a productive citizenry. Conflict becomes based in racial, cultural, or sexual differences that exclude the possibilities of common ground and compromise.

Church also taught Hedberg and many of the other subjects "how one should live" (Bellah et al., 1985, p. 239). Many subjects in this study mentioned how church and their religious or spiritual life was the underlying motivator or guide for public life. This reflects more of the idea of service that Coles (1993) spoke about in *The Call of Service: A Witness to Idealism*.

As an adult, Hedberg also discovered through her work that she was competent. She was able to achieve what no woman in her state had achieved; she had become a certified optometrist. The confidence she gained through developing her business and the importance of the community to the success of her business may have led to her involvement in her community.

Another common transference to the political arena is from success on the job to increased investment in community affairs. For many, the sense of being successful in work transmits to a feeling of obligation for community involvement and widens the number of memberships in work-related and community-oriented organizations. (Steckenrider & Cutler, 1989, p. 71)

Hedberg pointed out that this involvement in voluntary associations led her to an even greater appreciation for her capabilities.

The type of work one does has also been found to influence involvement in community life (Renshon, 1977, p. 96). Certain types of occupations provide not only prestige but also the skills necessary to be involved in community life (ibid.) Many of the subjects in this study had been or still are professional educators, an occupation that carries status as well as prepares individuals with the speaking and thinking skills necessary in public life.

Raising children, another "adult" role, involves individuals in community life. Parents, concerned about the play opportunities for their children, become more interested in recreational facilities available in the schools and in the community (Steckenrider & Cutler, 1989, p. 74). This leads to involvement in zoning and planning boards as well as the PTA and school boards. Many of the subjects in this study became involved in the community through the schools their children attended. They enjoyed this involvement, continued it, and, in some cases, became involved in other organizations.

FOCUS ON MICRO-SOCIOLOGY AND COMMUNITY POLITICS

An interesting feature of this study is that it focuses on voluntary activity within civil society that excludes political society. Most literature regarding political life in the social sciences, particularly political sociology, focuses on political attitudes and activities designed to influence the state. This research focuses on those behaviors that are directly related to one's own community and neighborhood.

In terms of socialization, this approach is perhaps more direct than a macro-sociological perspective. Human behavior is more likely to be influenced by primary groups and those secondary groups that are instrumental in the determination of rewards and punishments most significant to the individual. Therefore, in order to understand socialization, it is necessary to focus on more personal experiences and life histories rather than on abstract concepts of political theory.

By assuming this focus, this book has been able to provide a description of a model of citizenship that is grounded in community life and that promotes enlightened self-interest. These citizens are described as anticipating positive rewards when involved in social groups, including family and voluntary associations. They see themselves as part of a larger communal whole in which they play an important role. Subjects believe that public conflict must be settled in honest, open, rational debate, and that those individual political agendas concerned with power acquisition and money are discredited. The descriptions of the model citizens in this study can be used in further research on socialization to civil society and the various mediating institutions encompassed by it.

METHODOLOGY

While many of the findings in this research reflect the earlier work in the field of political socialization, the methodology took on a qualitative approach, because most of these former studies did not focus directly on the topic of socialization to civil society. While a qualitative research design is open to more insight and originality, it lacks generalizability. This was particularly true because of the homogeneity of the community studied. All of these subjects are of European-American descent, and most are either from working-class or middle-class families. The community itself is also somewhat unique in its history and development as an urban fringe area based around highly technological industries.

Other aspects of the research design could have been different and may have provided better results. Certainly a longitudinal panel study such as that done by Clausen (1993) would have provided much stronger results. However, there were other, less involved steps that could have improved the findings. For example, although the subjects in this study were identified by age and generally fit into one of two generations (World War II or baby boomers), a further stratification by age might have provided more information on the developmental sequences of civic careers. However, any analysis using age cohorts must consider the differing expectations of role behavior based on historical periods (Steckenrider & Cutler, 1989, p. 81).

Another approach that would have highlighted the findings of the study would have been to compare subjects who were not involved or did not reflect the model citizens studied here. The decision not to pursue this comparison concerned the multiple definitions of citizenship and identifying subjects. A random sample may consist of a variety of citizen models, some of which may have been the same as or different from my sample. Therefore, any comparison made on the assumption that these were two different groups (i.e., model active citizens and passive model citizens) would have been false. If I had intentionally chosen individuals who were not involved and who were opposite to my ideal citizen model, then there would have been a problem of identification.

How could this control group be identified out of all other citizens in the Town of Bedford, and how would these citizens be approached? If they were identified through the town property lists, I would have to call them and find out if they fit this antithetical model of citizenship. If they did fit this model, it is doubtful that they would want to participate, and they would most likely be insulted to be identified as such.

FACILITATING THE HEALTH OF CIVIL SOCIETY

Participation in civil society—if valued—needs to be promoted by the various agents of socialization: family, school, church, community, work, and so on. More than that, the culture and values of American life must promote active engagement in the social contexts in which we find ourselves. This requires the metastructures of corporate America and our national government to attempt to facilitate the growth of civil society.

First, our national economy must be designed to promote some stability of living and working within a community. It became clear that the subjects in this study came from stable communities where at least one generation of families was able to develop the community networks that strengthen child rearing. Relatively stable communities (i.e., one generation) offer the possibility for other adults to be involved in young people's lives. For the subjects in this book, this involvement helped promote educational motivation and led to a modeling of involvement that the subjects carry out in their communities today. This kind of stability requires that jobs in an area stay in an area for an extended period of time. This can only occur through a national economic policy and with corporate support.

Second, our state and national educational policy must support the holistic development of our young people. Young people need caring adults in their lives who can help them develop the skills and capacities necessary for a successful life. As Clausen (1993) suggests, we need to do our best to educate for planful competence. The findings in this study and in Clausen's work suggest that involvement in civil society is really about human development. If student success is measured by self-reliance or dependability, intellectual interest or involvement, and a belief in their need and capacity to act or self-confidence, then we can be relatively assured of their involvement in the public life of their community.

The subjects in this book reflected these characteristics. Most of the participants in this study were brought up to be responsible members of their families. Their contributions were important to the welfare of the family, and other family members depended on them. They were involved in organizations and activities that helped them realize their skills and develop them further. These interactions also influenced their value of social interaction to see their self-interest promoted by such interaction. The day-to-day practice of family discussions around the dinner table and the modeling of learning from parents promoted the intellectual curiosity necessary to an involved citizenry.

While much of this influence begins in the family, the practice of school life should try to further promote a sense of intellectual curiosity, competence, and self-reliance. This requires that schools have the resources to provide students with the attention they need to fully understand their talents and capabilities. Schools must also be able to support a variety of activities, so that involvement becomes an option for all students and not simply a minority. Students must have the opportunity to plan and to fail or succeed on their own. This is how they learn about responsibility, as was pointed out by the subjects in this study. Real responsibility means real consequences. Course work must be challenging and engaging. Students need to be able to articulate their ideas within a public setting and to learn how their ideas fit into a larger discourse about public good.

Lastly, schools need to be sure that there is a balance to ideas and practices that discriminate based on race, class, or gender.

For this group of homogeneous subjects, gender continued to be an issue. Women lacked opportunities for sports, external motivation for continuing education, and choices of career. The lack of these things may have limited their growth in some cases, but it may have also led to involvement in civil society in other cases, particularly as an outlet for their abilities and intellect. However, how much more might they have become capable of if they really had choices along the way? Perhaps they would have developed the skills and networks to become even more involved; perhaps they might have run for political office.

The opportunities for parental involvement in schools also served as a major factor for the involvement of the subjects in this study. Their interest in their own children brought them together with other community members to begin the social networks critical to civil society. This opportunity for involvement and local control of schools must be maintained. While certain state and national standards may be important to eliminate potential bias in the treatment of protected groups and to promote democratic citizenship, local boards should continue to set the agenda for the schools.

In the schools, students should be required to do service learning in one form or another. Community service occurs today mostly on a voluntary basis through local schools and colleges. Service learning requires students to perform community service but to reflect on this service. Mandatory service learning should reflect students' interests and skills but should deepen an understanding of taking responsibility as a member of a community, especially since students tend to focus on rights rather than on responsibilities (Harwood Group, 1993). Service learning has many benefits, not the least of which is to help students gain a better understanding of public issues and understand themselves as key participants in the well-being of others (Delve, Mintz, & Stewart, 1990). Performing service also tends to generate or heighten an interest in doing more service, as was demonstrated by the participants in this study.

The opportunities for service must also be promoted at a higher level. National government and corporate policy makers must try to promote community service. Some companies already foster community involvement with leave policies and flexible scheduling, as described by Chester Adams and by some of the other contacts I made during the research stage of this study. They worked for companies that allowed them to get involved in their communities by leaving early on some days and working later on others.

Governmental agencies must also learn to cooperate with local initiatives. Agencies should be rewarded for working with communities and not for enlarging their responsibilities. Agency personnel should learn how to facilitate community involvement and public problem solving and not try to keep local organizations out, as described by Phyllis Constantino. Larger agencies of the national government should only become engaged in community life when local agencies lack the appropriate resources or resolve.

The last concern is public space. At both a national and local level, the government must protect public space, including public education, public media, and public land. We must ensure that the pursuit of profit does not drive all of the mediating institutions that have such a great influence on our youth. Motivation around profit tends to limit the public's view of itself as client or consumer and not as active participant (Boyte, 1989). We also need to have public space in which to meet, socialize, debate, and resolve public issues. Such spaces were richly described by many of the subjects in this study. From playgrounds to town squares, participants in this research explained how such public spaces fostered a sense of belonging, provided an opportunity to know others and to be recognized, and promoted the development of the children in the community.

This book should provide some suggestions for further research on political socialization and civil society. Community studies and life histories are good approaches to understanding this process. However, further research into the individual agents of socialization and their influence in the community is needed. Families, churches, schools, the workplace, town boards, and the use of public space within a community all provide interesting avenues for research. The coming together of these agents, the historical events that shape people's attitudes, and the economic, social, and cultural practices of the time are all interrelated and significant to the understanding of socialization to civil society.

Appendix A

Random Phone Interview Guide

Peter Sawyer, Syracuse University
Interviews conducted in October 1995

Procedure:
I.   Using property title list provided by the Town Clerk, randomize list.
II.   Find random subjects and confirm primary residence by first noting difference between land value and total value.
        *need difference of $20,000 to confirm house built on property
        *if less, check other listings with same name below
        *if no possible residence or identified as business, follow down to next identifiable residence
        *write down name and confirm in local phone book residential listings
III. If confirmed, call and apply Interview Schedule below.

Interview Schedule:
(Note: These interviews were recorded.)
1.   What community do you currently live in?
      (to see how subjects identify with geographic and political boundaries, community identification)
2.   How well do you keep informed about local issues/news?
      (allow for self-report of internal validity)
3.   Are you aware of any voluntary organizations that regularly contribute to the welfare of your town/neighborhood?

(volunteer will be defined as non-paid activities which are freely entered
into) (this serves to identify organizations within community)

4.   Are you aware of any individual who volunteers, on a regular basis, to
     promote the welfare of your community/town/neighborhood?
     (this serves to identify individuals within community)

Note: As a cross-check in identifying subjects, frequency counts were kept on
the number of times an individual or organization was mentioned. Those that
were most frequently mentioned were selected.

Appendix B

Organizational Representative Interview Guide

Peter Sawyer, Syracuse University
Interviews conducted during November 1995

Interview Schedule:
1. Before we begin, I'd like to tell you a little about what I'm doing. This study is on civic virtue and political socialization. I'm trying to identify people who fit a particular form of citizenship and then interview them. Hopefully, this will provide some direction for civic education programs. I'd like to talk to you about what your church does in the way of volunteer service and to identify model citizens.
2. Before we begin, I need you to read and sign this. It is from the Institutional Review Board on Human Subjects at Syracuse University.
3. Thanks. Let's start off with your (organization). It was identified through a random phone survey as providing voluntary services to the community. People within the town seemed to identify with either the Village of Bedford or the lower part of the Town, Thomas Hills and Bedford Lake. What does your organization do in this area?
4. I'd like to ask you now about individuals. Are there specific people you can name who contribute a lot of time and energy to volunteer efforts in their community, who are aware of local news and issues, and who are able to keep their own self-interest within a broader public context?
5. Can you tell me what they do, or why you think they fit this model?
6. How would you like me to contact these people?

Appendix C

Identified Subjects
Interview Guide

Interviews took place between January and February 1996

Procedure:
Questioning began with general questions. The responses to these general questions were probed in areas that reflected the major concerns of the following interview schedule. In cases where the subject did not discuss topics, particularly those regarding major agents of socialization, they were asked later in the interview.

Interview Schedule:
1. Introductory Dialogue
   First of all, I'd like to thank you for taking the time to do this. I really believe that your contribution will make a difference in this study and in identifying ways to improve the preparation of young people for citizenship.
   As you can see, I'd like to record this interview. It is necessary for me to write down exactly what you say and not what I thought you said. Once I have completed the study, I will erase the tapes. Do you think that would be all right?
   Great. There's just one more technicality I need to follow before we begin. I need you to read the consent form and sign it. Thanks.
   Okay, let's get going then.
   (Note: These questions are somewhat based on subjects' schematic representations of self and local politics (see O'Neill's [1981] work "Cognitive Community Psychology" in *American Psychologist*, 36, 457–469.)

2. To begin, could you tell me about yourself?
   - looking for role descriptions, basic constructs for identity
   - follow up with any roles or identity constructs relevant to public life or the definition of political boundaries
   - if no mention of organizational or group activity, ask specifically about community involvement
3. Could you tell me about where you live?
   - don't give away anything; see how they choose to describe and define where they live
   - follow up with unclear responses
4. How are public issues resolved here?
   - looking for perceived political structure
   - probe for their involvement in organizational activity
   - see how structure makes sense with activity later

Questions on Mediating Institutions and Major Agents of Socialization
5. Ask that the subjects talk about family (orientation and procreation)
   - discussions, parental activity, sibling activity
6. Talk about peers
   - interests, activities
7. Talk about parents, education, and work life
8. Talk about school life
   - rules, classes, activities, mentors, how much
9. Talk about communities of orientation and procreation
   - how long lived in these communities
10. Talk about church life (if mentioned)
    - discussions, group involvement
11. Talk about work life
    - activities, decision making, group involvement of any kind

Additional Questions on Age Group and Life Course
12. What, if any, events shaped your thinking regarding public activities and political influence?
13. Do you see yourself as different from others of same age in terms of public life and politics? Why?
14. Can you think of anything else that may have influenced your thinking about public life (i.e., books, movies)?

Appendix D

Subject Biographies

ART FORBES (BORN 1918)

Art Forbes was born in 1918 to a farming family in the Village of Thomas Hills. He had one brother and four sisters. His "German" grandmother also lived with his family. At age fifteen, Forbes had to take over the responsibilities of the farm because his father died. He saw a stark contrast between his farm life and the life of other children in his town whose fathers worked for the railroad. On a farm, the priorities were always the animals first, school work second. Playtime revolved around the town's children creating their own fun without much parental involvement. Forbes said, "You had to make what you did, that's all."

School life involved small classes and close relations with his teachers. Teachers taught a variety of classes and supervised a number of extracurricular activities. One teacher, who was Forbes's science teacher and track coach, tried his best to help Forbes out. Since Forbes and one of his friends had expressed an interest in college, this teacher decided that they needed more training in chemistry. Forbes joked that the training was really an "experiment" involving the baking of cupcakes, none of which came out as expected.

Other adults in the community also took an interest in Forbes. Many of the farmers "paid attention to young people and their accomplishments." Forbes was once recognized for doing a good job of plowing a field, for example. His uncle, who was also the town supervisor, encouraged his interest in going to college. The connections of young people to other adults were greatly facilitated by farming traditions that brought the entire community together during harvest season to help one another.

Forbes worked on the farm while taking classes at local colleges. Eventually he was able to go to college full time, and he earned a degree in veterinarian medicine when he was thirty-one. After he graduated, he returned to Thomas Hills and established his own business. At that time, he was already married; he raised three children.

FRANK MICHAELS (BORN 1919)

Frank Michaels was born in 1919 in a town not too far from Bedford. He said that he lived in a "strictly blue-collar, white-overall" neighborhood, where everybody was "without a lot of money," but that there was "no real poverty." Many immigrants lived in the town, including English, Italians, and Scandinavians. As people moved into his neighborhood and built houses, the neighbors would often help. They would do what they could do or what they knew how to do.

His parents had also grown up in this town. His father was a "rabid union man," and Michaels enjoyed arguing with him on many issues. Both were very interested in politics. His father would often take him to local public meetings. His father worked as a bricklayer, and his mother "worked in the home" and occasionally as a pianist. His parents did not graduate from high school, but "were determined that their children were going to get a college education." However, the choice of course work and activities in Michaels's school was limited.

The area was growing so rapidly that there was a lack of educational resources. Fortunately, Michaels had "some great teachers." These teachers took an interest in him because he was a "good student." Many teachers came to Michaels's house and met with his parents to help get him into college. The teachers would also work with Michaels after school, providing him with additional course work that would help him get into college. Michaels did make it to college, and he was the first in his family to do so.

Originally, Michaels had planned to become a scientist. However, with the onset of World War II, he assumed that he would be in the military. He applied but was rejected by the air force. He found what he thought would be a temporary position teaching science at a local high school. He was never called into military service, and he said that "after three months of teaching, I knew where I belonged." He became very excited about teaching and eventually became a principal in a nearby town. After a few years as a principal and due to some local tension between different elements in the community, he decided to leave that position to become principal in the Town of Bedford.

Michaels married shortly after becoming a teacher, and he and his wife raised two children. During the interview, he talked about the differences between his childhood and that of his children's. He said that when he was young, children created their own activities, while his children had very structured activities, run either by the school or local associations run by other adults in the community.

CHARLES WITT (BORN 1926)

Charles Witt was born in 1926 in a town about two hours' south of Bedford near a major city. He was an only child, like his father, and he said that he had been "indulged or overindulged as a child." His parents were involved with many of his activities and were very "supportive." His father was involved with him in Boy Scouts, and his mother shared his love of reading.

His parents "encouraged [him] to keep busy." During the summer, he would go to a YMCA summer camp. Because of the war, Witt had to take on an unusual amount of responsibility in camp administration. Normally there would be college kids or other adults to help, but many were serving in the war or had to go through college as fast as possible. Witt also sang in the Christ Episcopal Church Choir. He made money singing in the choir and found the whole experience "a rigorous or well-organized procedure."

His parents also kept busy, often in war-related activities. Witt's mother volunteered in a program called "Buttons for Britain" from 1940 to 1941. The program sent warm clothes to the people in Britain who had lost their homes in the blitz. Witt's father was a short-wave radio operator and kept up with all of the information on the war. Radio was the dominant form of entertainment during this period, and Witt mentioned how his family and other families of the time would listen to the radio at night for news of the war.

The neighborhood he lived in was "fairly stable." He said that there was a "stability of relationships" with the people who lived in the neighborhood. When his grandmother, who was living with his family, was dying, Witt stayed with one of the neighbors. The neighborhood was also full of children who had their own "gangs." These gangs played together on their own in several of the vacant lots in the neighborhood.

Witt's parents had very clear expectations of his education. It had "been understood all along that [he] should go to college." However, he knew that he had to get a scholarship. He received a scholarship and went through a technical college in fourteen weeks due to the war schedule. Because of his impaired eyesight, he did not serve in the war. After he graduated, he went directly to work at Montauk Electric, a major source of employment in the Town of Bedford.

Witt met his wife on a blind date in college, and together they raised two children.

PETER DRISCOLL (BORN 1927)

Peter Driscoll was born in 1927 in Havensport, a small town on the coast of New England. He referred to it as a "small fishing town." Like Forbes, Driscoll had to take on a lot of responsibility very early in his life. He too had been raised on a farm, a dairy farm. When he was nine years old, his father had an accident and could no longer work the farm, so Driscoll and his brothers had to keep the farm going. During the war, Driscoll also had to patrol when he had "duty night." This meant that he had to look for enemy ships off the coast.

Driscoll's mother had been an inspiration to him. She had been a concert pianist until she too had an accident. She broke her fingers and was unable to play the piano again. However, she resolved to learn the organ and to continue to play music. Driscoll felt that this caused him to have great respect for his mother, and that she was someone "I had to look up to."

His involvement with his peers was always a large part of his life. He said that he was always very active, a leader and an organizer. He organized trips with his friends, played basketball, was involved in youth fellowship at his church, and was the class president. For him and for his generation, he felt that they shared something; they "were all going in the same direction."

While Driscoll had been enrolled in the air force after high school, the war ended before he went into active duty. When he came back from basic training, he went to the superintendent of the local school system to see if he could get into college. The superintendent told him that he had already registered him in college and that he only needed to take the entrance exam. Driscoll said, "[that] little act—it's something I'll never forget. I've always built up on that, to help people without them really asking me to help them." After he graduated from college in 1949, he was hired by Montauk Electric and moved to Bedford.

He married and helped raise three children. During the interview, he said that his basic philosophy is that "you'd like to leave this world better than when you entered it."

ROGER SMITH (BORN 1927)

Roger Smith was one of the most reluctant subjects when it came to discussing himself. As mentioned in chapter 4, he rarely elaborated on himself or his background. Much of what he had to say was in response to direct questions. The town he grew up in was a small farming community on the Canadian border. The house he lived in had been in his family since the 1880s and included his nuclear family, his father's mother, and his mother's aunt. He had one brother and one sister who were much older, fifteen and thirteen, respectively. At night the family would often be engaged in "stimulating discussions," particularly between his aunt and his father. During the summer, he spent much of his time at his mother's hometown on the New England coast.

His father was a lawyer and died when Roger was thirteen. He said that he did not "have any sense of loss of fellowship" when his father died, because he did not spend a lot of time with him. His father was a busy lawyer who was very active in the town, involved in the bridge club, the Kwanis Club, the Board of Education, the Republican Party, and the local church. Smith mentioned little about his mother.

Like many of the subjects in this study, he led a busy school life. He enjoyed school and was active in the stage club and choir. He had "a lot of memorable teachers" who were "there when you got there in the morning and were there as long as you wanted them in the afternoon."

After high school, Smith went on to college and worked for fourteen years in public schools. He then worked for Montauk Electric for many years before his retirement. He now is a mentor and a tutor for a state college that specializes in distance learning and nontraditional students. In comparing his volunteer work to politics, he said that he "would rather support and do whatever community building I guess that I choose to do in less spectacular ways."

ANNE SHARPE (BORN 1928)

Anne Sharpe originally grew up in a large metropolitan area and then moved into this area when she was a teenager. She spoke a lot about her family and the many troubles they faced. Her father had intensely disliked his job as a pressman and had lost several fingers due to it. He tried desperately to start his own business to get out of working as a pressman. Sharpe's mother tried to help him realize this dream, which resulted in her having little time for her children. Sharpe said: "She [her mother] was around but . . . she'd rush home, open some cans, and get supper. After a quick dinner, it was back to the business." Sharpe felt a special "void" in her relationship with her father. A year after they moved north, away from the city, her father died of cancer, perhaps intensifying this void.

Her mother was involved in several activities in the community, and Sharpe felt that that was "an important factor" in her own thinking about public life. She said that her mother was "a doer" and "a rebel," involved as an air raid volunteer during World War II, active in the local "Y" (YWCA/YMCA), and very involved in the church, even though she was not a member.

Sharpe felt that her home life "spilled over into school." She tended to daydream a lot and really did not have that many friends. Fortunately, many of the teachers really liked her and took a special interest in her, even bringing her into their homes. She had to quit school in her senior year due to an illness, and she and her family moved into this area shortly afterward.

When Sharpe moved here, she began to get involved in the church youth choir. Her peers in the choir encouraged her to return to school. She had strong academic interests in agriculture. However, when she got to college, her teachers did not envision a woman working on a farm, so they encouraged her to go into teaching. Eventually she graduated from college and went on to get a master's degree in school psychology.

She met her husband before she had completed college and decided that "in my own thinking, and in society, and certainly the husband's thinking," she would not go to "work." Instead, she became a full-time wife and mother. Today she works in many organizations and is particularly concerned with family issues. She places a high value on helping younger people.

CHUCK WALLACE (BORN 1928)

Chuck Wallace grew up in New England where he lived with his mother and father. He had one brother who was thirteen years younger and so "was not a factor in my life." His father had emigrated from Scotland and found a job as an hourly worker in an engineering department of a large business. He said that his mother was "a home person."

Both of his parents were very active in the community. They participated in bowling leagues, church, several Scottish organizations, and in a program that brought bandages to Britain. Wallace's father would always greet people at the door of their church and had helped start the first cub pack and later worked with the Boy Scouts. At one point, his dad also got involved with local politics, but he was "too darn . . . honest" to stay with it. Wallace felt that their involvement influenced him. He said: "As you're forming your personality, you were doing something for somebody else." At home, his father was very strict when it came to the rules of the house. He also encouraged his son to work hard at whatever he did.

Their neighborhood was made up of a lot of immigrants. Like their neighbors, Wallace's family did not have extended family, so there was a tendency to "adopt" other families within their community as relatives. He had many friends in the neighborhood and called them the "Vega Street Boys." Within the neighborhood, there was always a sense of safety. You also knew that if you did anything wrong, someone's mother would see you. They were "the watch dogs of the neighborhood."

Wallace was active both in school and outside of school. His main activities were sports, Boy Scouts, and church. He mentioned Boy Scouts as providing him with a sense of responsibility and how to work within an "organization framework." Church had always had a strong influence on him, and he met his wife in a youth group there. His two sons are named after former ministers of his church.

After high school, Wallace joined the marines. By joining he knew that he could go on to college through the GI bill. He said that otherwise he could not have afforded higher education. After he left the military, he went right into college and graduated with a two-year degree. He was hired by Montauk Electric and encouraged by his supervisor to continue his education, eventually earning both a bachelor's and a master's degree.

Wallace's decision to move to Bedford was based on information from a fellow worker. He found out that Bedford had a good school system and low taxes, and that he could get "more house for the money." When he moved here—much like the community he grew up in—he found that the community also seemed to become "like family." Many of the people were raising children and had also just moved into the area.

Wallace felt that he tends to be a leader because he has a good deal of self-confidence due to past success in leadership roles. He also said that he values being with others and has a real need to socialize with other people.

JAMES ROCKFORD (BORN 1930)

James Rockford grew up in the southern part of the state in a large metropolitan area. He described the community he grew up in as a "mixed community." He mentioned a substantial black community and a Jewish community, with the rest of the community made up of a mix, both ethnically and economically. He felt that this diversity helped to create a more open-minded person. Rockford's parents had emigrated from Sweden to the United States in the 1920s, and like other immigrants, they were on their own. His father worked in a maintenance department, and his mother worked nights for a lawyer. Although neither of his parents were involved in "civic activities," they were very involved with their friends. Their house "was one with which many people held their parties in."

Rockford felt that the school he attended was excellent and operated on the level of a junior college of today. "You were expected to work and perform." The social life of the community was outside of the school for Rockford and his friends. They belonged to fraternities and sororities that put on their own dances and other forms of entertainment. They did all of the planning and fund-raising and then shared the profits. After high school, he went on to college. He found that his high school had prepared him well, particularly for public speaking. He ended up doing a lot of public speaking in college and became very involved in different organizations.

Rockford married in 1952 and went to work for Montauk Electric. After several years, he began working in a consulting firm and eventually started his own woodworking business. When he moved into Bedford, he and his wife met several people through work, his neighborhood, and other organizations. They saw "other people doing things," so they saw their involvement as "the responsible thing to do," or "the right thing to do." Rockford said that "people ought to be contributing; we can't just be a taker." He mentioned a high value of independence or self-reliance. He and his wife have four children.

PHYLLIS CONSTANTINO (BORN 1938)

Phyllis Constantino's early memories of childhood—during the 1940s—are unclear or "not worth remembering." Her parents both struggled with alcoholism, and at age thirteen, she moved out, along with all of her siblings. She moved to a small town to live with her aunt and uncle. One of her brothers lived in the same town with her grandmother, and her other siblings lived with relatives in another town. She said that "the impact of having alcoholic parents and separating from her siblings affects her today."

Fortunately, Constantino's aunt and uncle took good care of her. Her uncle was the local mailman, and her aunt was a supervisor for the local office of a phone company. Her uncle "nurtured" her and "prepared her to go on" with her education. He helped both her and her brother go on to college. Her brother was also a major influence in her life. They had a close relationship, and even though he was only a year older, he was a "kind of parent figure" to her.

Since it was such a small town, everyone knew Constantino, her aunt, and her uncle. They were all well liked, and Constantino had a "good four years" when she lived in the town. She frequently spoke with many people in the town in her job at the "old-fashion soda fountain." She was also popular in school and was "part of the leaders of that high school." She said she was involved in numerous clubs and "social stuff."

Her teachers also lent her a lot of support. One encouraged her to go into nursing. He "fired something up, he really fired up science for me," Constantino said. While training to become a nurse, she had her first experience of "service." At her Catholic training hospital, "service" meant that one needed to view each patient as Jesus. She saw that the connection between this training and the ideals of service found in the Catholic church had a strong influence in her life.

When Constantino was older and had her own family, one priest in particular had an effect on her. This priest was good at getting people involved and "off their butt." She felt that he was the influence behind their taking more "ownership" of the activities of the church and of the problems in the community. The writings of Dorothy Day also encouraged her to provide service and to take "the next stage of the journey." "The journey" refers to her faith, which she feels is connected to her family, her community, and her church.

Constantino is married with two children and has both a bachelor's and a master's degree.

MICHAEL CONNERS (BORN 1940)

Mike Conners grew up in a small town during the 1940s. The experience of growing up in a small town had both "positive and negative aspects." On the positive side, he said that you always knew "what to expect from [your neighbors]." The downside was that in a small town there were not many places to go, and one had to "rely on the people in the community" for entertainment. He pointed out that television was not yet an option.

His father was the high school principal, and his mom looked after the house and the children. He felt that they did not have a lot—in a material sense—but that they were a close family. Since he was the principal of the school, Conners's father was very concerned with the public image his family carried. He had high expectations of his children, and Conners felt that this was why he was so involved. By getting involved in many organizations and activities, Conners could get some positive recognition from his father.

While Conners was busy in the informal life of the neighborhood children, he was also very involved in formal sports, school musical organizations, and church. Church provided really strong leadership activities for him and a "social environment with others." In his community, the church was also the organization that helped out when "the need arose." If somebody lost a barn, the community would organize through the church and build a new barn.

After high school, Conners went on to college. During college, he was influenced by the faculty and by a minister who took an interest in him. He enjoyed conversations with these individuals and felt that they had "shaped a lot of [his] thinking." To finance his education, Conners had to find numerous jobs. He said that he worked "99 hours a week" but really enjoyed being busy and "loved working with people."

He was drafted into the army and served in Vietnam before he came to Bedford, where he was hired to teach grade school. At the time I interviewed him, he had been married for thirty-four years and had raised three sons. One of his sons died of Hodgkin's disease a few years before. He still teaches and continues to enjoy it, because "the kids teach him things." He plans on retiring within the next few years.

TERRY NICOLS (BORN 1943)

Terry Nicols was raised in the 1940s and early 1950s in a nearby state. Her father had been a French Canadian who came to the United States to work in the mills. Her mother was Italian and was the first woman in the family to marry a non-Italian. The ethnic heritage of her family was quite strong, and English was a second language to both of her parents. She had two older brothers, a younger sister, and a younger brother. She described all of them as "a family of talkers."

Nicols's parents were both very involved in the community. Her father was a town councilman, and her mother was "a doer, a helper." Nicols felt that they had influenced her to become involved in the same way that she hopes she has influenced her children. "I think you learn without even thinking. You're learning by observing what goes on in your family. I would expect, at some point, my children are likely to become involved in organizations and to be able to do things in their community."

The Catholic church also played a significant role in her life. Nicols felt that through home and church "you learn . . . that society has different expectations of your behavior." She went to Catholic schools until ninth grade, when her parents gave her a choice of schools. She elected to go the local public school, which she believed to be a better school both academically and in terms of activities. In reference to her school life, Nicols described herself as a "typical, introverted, shy person who then becomes talkative and a doer." She was involved in sports, chorus, the debate club, and other activities.

When she graduated from high school, Nicols was able to attend a private women's college in the area. The college had a special program for commuting students—tuition was one-quarter the regular cost if one lived at home. While Nicols enjoyed her education there, she often felt like an outsider. She said that the good teachers were the ones who gave the students "tools for thinking," and that they "opened up your mind."

She raised two children with her husband, and said, "she doesn't have to work." Before she had children, Nicols had worked as a social worker and a recreational therapist. At the time of the interview, she was considering returning to work.

MARY HEDBERG (BORN 1946)

Mary Hedberg was brought up in the late 1940s and early 1950s. Her upbringing was very troubled. She stated that her parents did not want her, and that only their religious beliefs—they were Catholic—kept her mother from having an abortion. Hedberg had three siblings, one of which also shared her problem of parental disinterest. Despite her parents' attitudes toward her or, more likely, because of it, Hedberg was motivated to prove herself worthy.

Her parents had not expected her to go on to college and had hoped that she would marry. Hedberg struggled with school when she was young, perhaps due to her parents' negative influence. As an adult, however, she found that she could be a good student. Eventually she went on to pass a state certification and became the first woman—without a male backer—in the state to become an optometrist.

Hedberg felt that the Catholic church countered some of the negative influences that her parents had had on her. She said that her parents were particularly adept at "fault finding" along racial lines. The church provided an alternative view to these perceptions, and, since "much of what her parents said was wrong," she was more open to what the church said about these issues. "I think that, through the church, you can claim yourself, you can get satisfaction from, you can give, get, or receive a value system that doesn't necessarily have to relate to your value system as a child."

The success of her own business and her desire to continue to learn provide the basis for her volunteer work. Hedberg is married with two children.

KATHY MADISON (BORN 1950)

Kathy Madison lived on a lake in the Town of Bedford. I interviewed her in her home. She grew up in the 1950s on Long Island, New York. Her father was an attorney, and her mother worked in the home to raise her three children, of which Madison was the oldest. Her mother, born in Germany, was described as "a very brilliant person." As a woman, there were no parental or societal expectations or encouragement for her to go to college. She graduated from high school at age fifteen and became a legal secretary. Before her children were born, she had worked outside of the home in that position, and after they were raised, she did the same. Madison's father was an attorney. She did not talk about him all that much but did mention that he was an alcoholic.

Madison described her community as a small town that was "safe and clean." The town had a mix of people from different economic classes, but most of Madison's friends were upper class to upper-middle class. She felt that some of the material values that some of her wealthier friends exhibited were "not appropriate." She felt very safe in her community and mentioned that the main street "had a lot of shops and fun things to do."

Madison was very active with her "group," a name that describes a number of friends with whom she spent her time. This group tended to do very well in school and to be very active. Madison was involved in sports, drama, music, and dances after school. The public high school she attended was "very good" and had a variety of courses and opportunities for students. Like many of the subjects, Madison felt that she had some really good teachers, one who encouraged her to write and to get things published at a young age. She said that great teachers were "the kind of people who called a spade a spade and didn't take a lot of anything from any kid but really, really loved the kids." Her church life was "very stiff and formal," and it was "more ritual than doing things for other people."

Two of the key mentors in Madison's life were her grandmother and her cousin. She said that her grandmother "did a lot of things for people" and "assumed the best in everybody." Her cousin had "a really neat spirit." "She had that spirit of going through life like I can do anything." Madison mentioned that her cousin would take weird courses, wear weird clothes, and sneak out of her house at night, and that she was a good person. She said that her cousin's early death at age twenty-nine had a large impact on her.

Today Madison is married with three children. She says that her husband and his family have been a "very big influence" in her adult life. Their ideas on friendship and entertaining were more informal and relaxed. Madison teaches in a nearby school district and continues to be a strong advocate for children in that district as well as in her home school district. She helps kids with clothing or school supplies and says of her volunteer work that she enjoys working other people: that she is a "people person."

ANDREA CALIFANO (BORN 1951)

I met Andrea Califano at her home, which is just outside the Town of Bedford. Califano was raised in the 1950s in a nearby state. Her father worked for the local department of motor vehicles, and her mother was a recovery room nurse for one of the hospitals in the area. She said that while her parents were not involved in the community, they were "always giving to other people, they would always help anybody out." Califano had an older sister and a younger brother. Since her mother worked night shifts, she had to take on many of the responsibilities of the house. Her parents were also very strict. Califano thought that that had helped her become "a stronger person." "You weren't allowed to go along with the crowd. And I think that makes you stronger; it makes you a stronger character."

She said that she did not have a lot of close friends, but that she was very active in school. She served on the prom committee and was involved in "junior achievement." Although Califano wanted to play sports, at the time sports were only for men. She enjoyed her classes and found her teachers very supportive. She mentioned one class in particular—"Problems in Democracy." She said that she liked to "get up and talk," and that "everything was allowed . . . you could voice your opinion and not get in trouble for it." Her schooling was mostly Catholic, and she mentioned that this particular teacher was not a nun.

Church life was very significant to Califano. Her parents "instilled" in her that "it was important to support your church." She said of her faith that it is "helping other people; also doing what I can to help humanity."

She went on to college and earned a bachelor's degree in home economics education. She had planned on going on for her master's but changed her mind when she got married. Califano chose to stay home to raise her two children. She places a high value on marriage and family and feels that many people today put more emphasis on material values than on raising children.

JAN HYLAND (BORN 1951)

Jan Hyland was born in the early 1950s in a small town a half hour from Bedford. She was raised in farmland, although she herself did not live on a farm. Her father worked as a time study engineer, and her mom was a "stay at home mom" until Hyland was in the fifth grade. Her mom then began to work as a part-time nursery school teacher. She said that her rural upbringing emphasized closeness to family. Her mother was herself very "family oriented." Hyland was the youngest of four kids and looked up to and competed with her older siblings. One of the consequences was that she grew up never being afraid to speak her mind.

Like many of those identified, Hyland was very active in school and quite successful in academics. She was valedictorian of her class and participated in school governance, intramural sports, drama, and several other clubs and organizations. She said of her activities that she "stayed after school virtually all the time, because that was the fun part of school. I remember having the feeling that, as an adolescent, that that was the thing that made school worthwhile."

In regard to her academics, Hyland said that she was a very compliant female. This, combined with being a "good test taker," allowed for her "academic success." She spoke about how the media and the music of the time stereotyped the role of women in society as "being tied up with the man she married or whose ring she was wearing or whatever." Hyland went on to college and continued to be involved there. Some of the experiences that she had in college helped her become aware of her skills and competencies as a leader and an organizer.

Church was also a major influence in Hyland's life. She said that it was not so much her parents' insistence on her church involvement, but that it was "just part of who I am, so I do that." She was involved in the youth group in school and was recognized by the church community for her efforts in helping to build a church camp.

Hyland has two children and places a high value on marriage and family. She also values her commitments and responsibilities to organizations. She says that she needs to "believe a purpose beyond myself is real important rather than just the day-to-day, hand-to-mouth kind of living that, or just accumulating things."

LINDA SIMMONS (BORN 1952)

Linda Simmons grew up in the 1950s and early 1960s in a community around twenty miles from the Town of Bedford. While the community was mostly rural, in the late 1950s a number of young families with children moved into the town. She enjoyed her childhood but found herself to be the only female in her neighborhood. She said that this small community gave her a sense of security.

Her father was from the area, as was his father. Her grandfather had graduated from college and worked in a local mill until it closed down during the depression. Her father never completed his high school degree but became a salesman and was "on the road" a lot. Often the family would only see him at dinner. Simmons had a younger brother and a younger sister.

Her mother had moved into the area when she was in high school, where she met Simmons's father and married him. Her mother and grandmother were very involved in their community and were always able to stand up in public and argue for their beliefs. Simmons saw this as being quite different from other women of their time.

The friends she made at school all tended to be more academically inclined. In fact, Simmons laughed at how she had been "a better student, because [she] had them for friends." She said that she was more "physical, let's go out and do something kind of thing."

After school Simmons went to a local community college, where a lot of her high school classmates went. She then began to commute to a local state college, but her parents had problems paying for it, so she had to go part time. She married around this time and stopped going to college, because it "became less of an issue." Later on, she began working part time in marketing, and the experience convinced her to go back for her degree.

CHESTER ADAMS (BORN 1955)

Chester Adams was one of three subjects who grew up in this community. He described the community as being "very close." He talked about how the neighbors would always help one another, and how they would regularly come together on a social basis. Adams contrasted this with other communities and distinguished his community from "the very suburban" people who are "from outside the area."

His father was an electrician with some additional technical training, and his mother had a background in early childhood education. She worked as a nursery school teacher for awhile and then worked in a nursing home to coordinate volunteer efforts. Adams had one sister, and everyone in the family was active in 4H, a local agricultural organization for young people, and all attended church on a regular basis.

Adams now teaches emergency care at a local community college and volunteers a good deal of his time as a paramedic, mostly at youth sports games. He finds that many people do not understand why he spends so much of his time as a volunteer; they feel that he should get paid for this work. He believes that many people spend some time in voluntary activities, and those that do not are unable to see any benefit in it.

He is married with two children.

TODD BUELLER (BORN 1956)

Todd Bueller grew up in and "never ventured outside" of the Town of Bedford. This made him a "hometown boy" or, because he lived on the lake, a "lake resident." Like Adams, Bueller saw a distinction between hometown people and "outsiders," primarily those who had recently moved into the area.

Bueller grew up in a large family. He had three brothers and four sisters. They all got along very well. He said, "You didn't have to worry about having friends over to entertain you," because they would do everything as a family. In fact, he said that they did not do much at all in the community, because they did do everything as a family. He did not talk about his mother very much but did mention his father several times.

Bueller said that his father was involved in several community and political organizations when he was younger but had to stop these activities to work overtime and support his family. Once the children were older, his father became involved again in an organization that worked for the improvement of the lake community, and he also was involved in the Democratic Party. Bueller said his father was very aware of local, national, and international news, a habit Bueller keeps to this day.

His own involvement in the fire department was influenced by a television series on emergency crews, his natural inclination to help people, and his brothers' involvement. His two older brothers had joined the fire department as soon as they were eighteen, and both had been chiefs of the fire department at one point.

Bueller is married with three children.

OSCAR THOMAS (BORN 1957)

Oscar Thomas grew up in a large city in the state. He came from a neighborhood where there was a high population density. He said that the neighbors were very close in their relations with one another. Families would share child care responsibilities, and everyone "kept an eye out" for the kids in the neighborhood.

Thomas had five brothers and sisters. His oldest brother, with whom he shared a room, had the biggest impact. This brother ran away from home when Thomas was quite young. The brother came back years later, but Thomas never got over him leaving him and his family. His mother was someone with whom Thomas could always talk. She taught him to take on responsibility for himself at an early age, because he was diagnosed with diabetes when he was very young. His mother tried to teach all of her kids to be both independent and responsible around the house. Both of Thomas's parents encouraged him to do well in school. They themselves set an example, as they both went back to school later in life and worked quite hard to get good grades.

Thomas went to Catholic school until the tenth grade. He then went to public school, where he found many more opportunities to get involved in music, art, and sports. His involvement in sports was very important to him.

Besides school, the Catholic church had a large influence on his life. Thomas said that this background taught him that "we're not here only for ourselves, but we're here to serve others." He also said that he's "always felt the direct impact I've had on others allowed me to feel that I'm able to serve others."

What Thomas had learned from the church affected him later on as an adult and led to his getting involved in civil society. His first involvement came in reaction to the Gulf War during the Bush administration. He felt that the war stood in contrast to the values he had been taught in church. Thomas also felt that, as a father, he could not stand by while "innocent people were going to get killed and maimed." After this experience, he felt a need to get involved in politics at a local level. He felt that his running for the school board was a reflection of that.

Thomas's comments here are strikingly similar to de Tocqueville's view on how broader political involvement can lead to local concern. "In politics, men combine for great undertakings, and the uses they make of the principle of association in important affairs practically teaches them that it is their interest to help one another in those of less moment" (1848/1990, p. 116).

Thomas did run for the school board and has served on that board for several years. He has now lived in this community for about twenty years. While he does not find it as close as the community he grew up in, he does find that the road he lives on is "a little community." Today he helps coordinate advisement services for a state agency. At this agency, he helps people find their "niche" and "find their way."

Thomas is married with two children.

Appendix E

Written Consent Form

WRITTEN CONSENT FORM*

Please review the following and sign at the bottom if you agree to the taping of this interview.

I. This study is designed to identify how model citizens think about their activities and, secondly, to identify what experiences, events, and/or influences lead to civic behavior. This will be used to provide direction for civic education programs. During this interview, you will have the opportunity to reflect on your life and make connections between your life history and how it shapes your behaviors today.

II. While there is some structure to the interview, you are encouraged to discuss whatever strikes you as significant to your thinking and behavior in community life. With your permission, these interviews will be recorded. After the study is completed, the tapes will be erased.

III. Your identity will remain confidential. The interviewer will be the only one who will know who you are, and any reports or publications that come from this study will maintain your anonymity.

IV. Your participation in this study is voluntary, and you may withdraw at any time without prejudice.

V. You may only participate if you are 18 years of age or older.

---

* Note that the original consent forms were on Department of Social Science letterhead.

After you have read the five statements above and have agreed to allow a tape recording of this interview, please sign below and print your name.

Signed _____

Print _____

Researcher: Peter R. Sawyer
              Department of Social Science
              Maxwell School
              Syracuse University

Notes

CHAPTER 1

1. Civil society is the voluntary space that exists between the individual and the state. For further explanation please refer to chapter 2.

2. Putnam (1993, p. 163; emphases in original) outlines four situations in which citizens within a democratic community or state should cooperate but do not. They are:

1. In the *tragedy of the commons*, no herder can limit grazing by anyone else's flock. If he limits his own use of the common meadow, he alone loses. Yet unlimited grazing destroys the common resource on which the livelihood of all depends.

2. A *public good*, such as clean air or safe neighborhoods, can be enjoyed by everyone, regardless of whether he contributes to its provision. Under ordinary circumstances, therefore, no one has an incentive to contribute to providing the public good, and too little is produced, causing all to suffer.

3. In the dismal *logic of collective action*, every worker would benefit if all struck simultaneously, but whoever raises the strike banner risks betrayal by a well-rewarded scab, so everyone waits, hoping to benefit from someone else's foolhardiness.

4. In *the prisoner's dilemma*, a pair of accomplices is held incommunicado, and each is told that if he alone implicates his partner, he will escape scot-free, but if he remains silent, while his partner confesses, he will be punished especially severely. If both remained silent, both would be let off lightly, but unable to coordinate their stories, each is better off squealing, *no matter what the other does.*

CHAPTER 2

1. Meaning refers to a process by which individuals interpret the symbols in their environment, generating contexts for their responses. This term is based on the work of Blumer (1969) and symbolic interactionism.

2. Voluntary associations are those organizations made up of volunteers (nonpaid), whose purpose is to do some public good. This excludes business corporations and other economic associations. See Berger and Neuhaus (1996).

3. "A primary group consists of a small number of people who regularly interact on a face-to-face basis, have close personal ties, and are emotionally committed to the relationship" (Thompson & Hickey, 1994).

4. This perspective echoes Jeffersonian values of agricultural life and the formation of character.

CHAPTER 3

1. Verba, Schlozman, and Brady (1995) solicited these responses by asking the question about membership in an organization, "for example, unions or professional associations, fraternal groups, recreational organizations, political issue organizations, community and school groups, and so on" (see their footnote 11 on p. 62).

2. As an example, Ogbu (1990) states that ". . . blacks sometimes interpret the school rules and standard practices as impositions of a white cultural frame of reference which do not necessarily meet their 'real educational needs'" (p. 81).

3. In referring to family here, I am using the term to refer only to those intimate social groups in which the raising of children is a goal or practice of the adults, adults who also have some form of commitment to one another.

CHAPTER 4

1. The Town of Bedford is a fictitious name, as are all locations given in this book, to help provide confidentiality to the subjects in this research.

CHAPTER 5

1. The World War II generation refers to those born around World War I and roughly before the 1940s. The baby boom generation generally refers to those born shortly after the end of World War II and before the end of the early 1960s.

2. Dionne (1991) explains that this disinterest in national politics is partly due to the character of the American political system. Contemporary power structures and party organizations articulate positions that are not reflective of the needs and values of the American people. Greider (1992) further argues that the electoral system in the United States is structured around the interests of those who have resources and who can contribute to campaigns. These people can therefore influence which representatives are available to the electorate.

3. Califano lives in Smithton Meadows, a town just west of Bedford. Her neighborhood is on the border of the town, and she attends church in the Town of Bedford.

4. Subsidiarity refers to "assigning social tasks to the smallest social unit that can perform them adequately" (Glendon & Blankenhorn, 1995, p. 10). The concept is further developed in the National Conference of Catholic Bishops (1986).

CHAPTER 6

1. Community has, indeed, a variety of definitions. In this research, community should be understood as that social group in which individuals develop a sense of their own identity (see Sandel, 1996) and that provides a context for moral meaning.

2. Putnam (1993) argues that these social contacts, or what he calls "vibrancy of associational life," are critical to the creation of a civic community. Civic communities are those communities that best supported regional governments in his study of Italy.

References

Almond, G., & Verba, S. (1963). *The civic culture.* Boston: Little, Brown.

Ansley, F., & Gaventa, J. (1997, January/February). Researching for democracy and democratizing research. *Change, 29,* 46–53.

Bandow, D. (1994). Libertarian: Building civil society through virtue and freedom. In D. E. Eberly (Ed.), *Building a community of citizens: Civil society in the 21st century* (pp. 319–332). New York: University Press of America.

Barber, B. (1980). *"Mass apathy" and voluntary social participation in the United States.* New York: Arno Press.

Barber, B. R. (1984). *Strong democracy: Participatory politics for a new age.* Berkeley: University of California Press.

Barber, B. R. (1995, Spring). Searching for civil society. *National Civic Review, 84,* 114–118.

Baumgartner, M. P. (1988). *The moral order of a suburb.* New York: Oxford University Press.

Beck, P. (1977). The role of agents in political socialization. In S. A. Renshon (Ed.), *Handbook of political socialization: Theory and research* (pp. 115–141). New York: Free Press.

Bellah, R. N., Madsen, R., Sullivan, W. M., Swidler, A., & Tipton, S. M. (1985). *Habits of the heart: Individualism and commitment in American life.* New York: Harper & Row.

Bellah, R. N., Madsen, R., Sullivan, W. M., Swidler, A., & Tipton, S. M. (1992). *The good society.* New York: Vintage Books.

Berger, P. L., & Neuhaus, R. J. (1996). *To empower people: From state to civil society* (2nd ed.). Washington, DC: AEI Press.

Berkowitz, W. (1987). *Local heroes: The rebirth of heroism in America.* Lexington, MA: Lexington Books.

Blumer, H. (1969). *Symbolic interactionism: Perspective and method.* Englewood Cliffs, NH: Prentice-Hall.

Bogdan, R. C., & Biklen, S. K. (1992). *Qualitative research for education: An introduction to theory and methods.* Boston: Allyn and Bacon.

189

Boyte, H. (1989). *Commonwealth: A return to citizen politics.* New York: Free Press.

Boyte, H. (1994). Populist: Citizen as public work and public freedom. In D. E. Eberly (Ed.), *Building a community of citizens: Civil society in the 21st century* (pp. 333–354). New York: University Press of America.

Carlson, A. C. (1994). Traditionalist: Strengthening the bonds of civil society. In D. E. Eberly (Ed.), *Building a community of citizens: Civil society in the 21st century* (pp. 293–304). New York: University Press of America.

Chaffee, S. H., with Jackson-Beek, M., Durall, J., & Wilson, D. (1977). Mass communication in political socialization. In S. A. Renshon (Ed.), *Handbook of political socialization: Theory and research* (pp. 223–258). New York: Free Press.

Clausen, J. (1993). *American lives: Looking back at the children of the great depression.* New York: The Free Press.

Cohen, J. (1995). Interpreting the notion of civil society. In M. Walzer (Ed.), *Toward a global civil society* (pp. 35–40). Providence, RI: Berghahn Books.

Coles, R. (1987). *The political life of children.* Boston: Houghton Mifflin.

Coles, R. (1993). *The call of service: A witness to idealism.* New York: Houghton Mifflin.

Conner, R. L. (1994). Communitarian: A new balance between rights and responsibilities. In D. E. Eberly (Ed.), *Building a community of citizens: Civil society in the 21st century* (pp. 305–318). New York: University Press of America.

Cook, K., Fine, G., & House, J. (1995). *Sociological perspectives on social psychology.* Boston: Allyn and Bacon.

Daloz, L., Keen, C., Keen, J., & Parks, S. (1996). *Common fire: Leading lives of commitment in a complex world.* Boston: Beacon Press.

Daly, M. (1994). *Communitarianism: A new public ethics.* Belmont, CA: Wadsworth.

Dass, R. (1985). *How can I help?* New York: Knopf.

Davies, J. (1977). Political socialization: From womb to childhood. In S. A. Renshon (Ed.), *Handbook of political socialization: Theory and research* (pp. 142–171). New York: Free Press.

Delve, C., Mintz, S., & Stewart, G. (Eds.). (1990). *Community service as values education.* San Francisco: Jossey-Bass.

Derber, C. (1996). *The wilding of America: How greed and violence are eroding our nation's character.* New York: St. Martin's Press.

De Tocqueville, Alexis de. (1848/1990). *Democracy in America.* New York: Vintage Books.

Dionne, Jr., E. J. (1991). *Why Americans hate politics.* New York: Simon & Schuster.

Dye, T. (1995). *Who's running America* (6th ed.). Englewood Cliffs, NJ: Prentice Hall.

Eberly, D. E. (1994). *Building a community of citizens: Civil society in the 21st century.* New York: University Press of America.

Elshtain, J. B. (1995). *Democracy on trial.* New York: Basic Books.

Etzioni, A. (1996). *The new Golden Rule: Community and morality in a democratic society.* New York: Basic Books.

Ferguson, A. (1971). *An essay on the history of civil society.* New York: Garland.

Galston, W. (1991). *Liberal purposes: Goods, virtues, and duties in the liberal state.* Cambridge: Cambridge University Press.

Gay, L. R. (1996). *Educational research: Competencies for analysis and application* (5th ed.). Englewood Cliffs, NJ: Prentice Hall.

Glendon, M., & Blankenhorn, D. (Eds.). (1995). *Seedbeds of virtue: Sources of competence, character, and citizenship in American society.* New York: Madison Books.

Goffman, I. (1959). *The presentation of self in everyday life.* New York: Doubleday.

Goffman, I. (1961). *Asylums: Essays on the social situation of mental patients and other inmates.* New York: Doubleday.

Greider, W. (1992). *Who will tell the people: The betrayal of American democracy.* New York: Simon & Schuster.

Hall, J. (1995). In search of civil society. In J. A. Hall (Ed.), *Civil society: Theory, history, comparison* (pp. 1–31). Cambridge: Polity Press.

Harwood Group. (1993). *College students talk politics.* New York: The Kettering Foundation.

Hearn, F. (1997). *Moral order and social disorder.* New York: Aldine De Gruyter.

Hummel, R. P. (1980). *Politics for human beings.* Monterey, CA: Duxbury Press.

Hunter, Floyd. (1963). *Community power structure.* Garden City, NY: Doubleday.

Hyman, H. H. (1959). *Political socialization: A study in the psychology of political behavior.* Glencoe, IL: Free Press.

Kymlicka, W., & Norman, W. (1997). Return of the citizen: A survey of recent work on citizenship theory. In R. Braungart, B. Dayton, L. Eastwood, A. Meleshevich, M. Rupert, M. Stanley, M. Thompson, M. Voorheis, K. Walker, & D. Wharton (Eds.), *Critical issues for the United States: The American Dream reconsidered* (pp. 1–40). New York: McGraw-Hill.

Lasch, C. (1978). *The culture of narcissism: American life in an age of diminishing expectations.* New York: Norton.

Levine, A. (1993, September/October). The making of a generation. *Change, 25,* 8–15.

Loeb, P. (1999). *Soul of a citizen: Living with conviction in a cynical time.* New York: St. Martin's Griffin.

Macedo, S. (1990). *Liberal virtues: Citizenship, virtue, and community.* Oxford: Oxford University Press.

Marshall, T. H. (1965). *Class, citizenship, and social development.* New York: Anchor.

McNeil, L. M. (1988). *Contradictions of control.* New York: Routledge.

Mills, C. W. (1956). *The power elite.* New York: Oxford University Press.

Mills, C. W. (1959). *The sociological imagination.* London: Oxford University Press.

Nathan, J., & Remy, R. (1977). Comparative political socialization: A theoretical perspective. In S. A. Renshon (Ed.), *Handbook of political socialization: Theory and research* (pp. 85–111). New York: Free Press.

National Conference of Catholic Bishops. (1986). *Economic justice for all: Pastoral letter on Catholic social teaching and the U.S. economy.* Washington, DC: National Conference of Catholic Bishops.

Novak, M. (1995). The cultural roots of virtue and character. In D. E. Eberly (Ed.), *The content of America's character: Recovering civic virtue* (pp. 47–62). New York: Madison Books.

Ogbu, J. (1990). Overcoming racial barriers to equal access. In T. I. Goodlad & P. Keating (Eds.), *Access to knowledge: An agenda for our nation's schools* (pp. 59–89). New York: The College Board.

O'Neill, P. (1981). Cognitive community psychology. *American Psychologist, 36,* 457–469.

Orum, A. M. (1989). *Introduction to political sociology: The social anatomy of the body politic* (3rd ed.). Englewood Cliffs, NJ: Prentice Hall.

Patrick, J. J. (1977). Political socialization and political education in schools. In S. A. Renshon (Ed.), *Handbook of political socialization: Theory and research* (pp. 190–222). New York: Free Press.

Perez-Diaz, V. (1995). The possibility of civil society: Traditions, character, and challenges. In J. A. Hall (Ed.), *Civil society: Theory, history, comparison* (pp. 80–109). Cambridge: Polity Press.

Phillips, K. (1990). *The politics of rich and poor: Wealth and the american electorate in the Reagan aftermath.* New York: HarperCollins.

Postman, N. (1985). *Amusing ourselves to death: Public discourse in an age of show business.* New York: Viking Press.

Putnam, R. D. (1993). *Making democracy work: Civic traditions in modern Italy.* Princeton: Princeton University Press.

Renshon, S. A. (Ed.). (1977). *Handbook of political socialization: Theory and research.* New York: Free Press.

Renshon, S. A. (1990). Educating political leaders in a democracy. In O. Ichilov (Ed.), *Political socialization, citizen education, and democracy* (pp. 313–345). New York: Teachers College Press.

Sandel, M. (1996). *Democracies discontent: America in search of a public philosophy.* Cambridge: Belknap Press of Harvard University Press.

Sanderson, S. K. (1995). *Macrosociology: An introduction to human societies.* New York: HarperCollins.

Scott, T. (1990). *The rating guide to life in America's small cities.* Buffalo: Prometheus Books.

Seidel, J., Friese, S., & Leonard D. (1995). *The enthograph v4.0: A user's guide.* Amherst, MA: Qualis Research Associates.

Sigel, R. (Ed.). (1970). *Learning about politics: A reader in political socialization.* New York: Random House.

Sigel, R. (Ed.). (1989). *Political learning in adulthood: A sourcebook of theory and research.* Chicago: University of Chicago Press.

Sigel, R., & Hoskin, M. (1977). Perspectives on adult political socialization—Areas of research. In S.A. Renshon (Ed.), *Handbook of political socialization: Theory and research* (pp. 259–293). New York: Free Press.

Silbiger, S. L. (1977). Peers and political socialization. In S. A. Renshon (Ed.), *Handbook of political socialization: Theory and research* (pp. 172–189). New York: Free Press.

Stacey, B. (1977). *Political socialization in western society: An analysis from a life-span perspective.* New York: St. Martin's Press.

Stack, C. (1975). *All our kin: Strategies for survival in a black community.* New York: Harper & Row.

Steckenrider, Jamie S., & Cutler, Neal E. (1989). Aging and adult political socialization: The importance of roles and transitions. In R. S. Sigel (Ed.), *Political learning in adulthood: A sourcebook of theory and research* (pp. 56–88). Chicago: University of Chicago Press.

Strauss, A. (1987). *Qualitative analysis for social scientists.* Cambridge: Cambridge University Press.

Thompson, W. E., & Hickey, J. V. (1994). *Society in focus: An introduction to sociology.* New York: HarperCollins.

Tussman, J. (1997). The office of citizen. In R. Braungart, B. Dayton, L. Eastwood, A. Meleshevich, M. Rupert, M. Stanley, M. Thompson, M. Voorheis, K. Walker, & D. Wharton (Eds.), *Critical issues for the United States: The American Dream reconsidered* (pp. 104–111). New York: McGraw-Hill.

U.S. Bureau of the Census (1992). *1990 census of population and housing.* Washington, DC: U.S. Dept. of Commerce, Economics and Statistics Administration, Bureau of the Census.

Van Gennep, A. (1960). *The rites of passage.* (M. B. Vizedom & G. L. Caffee, Trans.). Chicago: University of Chicago Press.

Verba, S., Schlozman, K. L., & Brady, H. E. (1995). *Voice and equality: Civic voluntarism in American politics.* Cambridge: Harvard University Press.

Walzer, M. (1992). *What it means to be an American.* New York: Marsilio.

Walzer, M. (Ed.). (1995). *Toward a global civil society.* Providence, RI: Berghahn Books.

Weissberg, R., & Joslyn, R. (1977). Methodological appropriateness in political socialization research. In S. A. Renshon (Ed.), *Handbook of political socialization: Theory and research* (pp. 45–84). New York: Teachers College Press.

Woshinsky, O. (1995). *Culture and politics.* Englewood Cliffs, NJ: Prentice Hall.

Index